Faith Beyond Reason

Other titles in the Reason and Religion series:

Peter Byrne: *The Moral Interpretation of Religion*

Stephen T. Davis: *God, Reason and Theistic Proofs*

Paul Helm: *Faith And Understanding*

Faith Beyond Reason

A Kierkegaardian Account

C. Stephen Evans

William B. Eerdmans Publishing Company
Grand Rapids, Michigan / Cambridge, U.K.

To Kelley
With hope that her faith will continue
to grow and deepen

Published jointly 1998 in the United States of America by
Wm. B. Eerdmans Publishing Company
255 Jefferson Ave. S.E., Grand Rapids, Michigan 49503
and in the U.K. by Edinburgh University Press
22 George Square, Edinburgh

Printed in the United States of America

02 01 00 99 98 5 4 3 2 1

ISBN 0-8028-4555-X

Contents

Preface

'Faith's conflict with the world is not a battle of thought with doubt, thought with thought . . . Faith . . . is a battle of character.'[1] Part of the genius of the Danish philosopher-theologian Søren Kierkegaard (1813–55) was a sure grasp of the idea that faith is not primarily intellectual in nature. In Kierkegaard's language, faith is a passion, and the passions are enduring traits that shape a person's character. However, it does not follow from the fact that faith is not primarily intellectual that it does not have intellectual consequences. Nor did Kierkegaard think this was so. He maintains, in fact, that faith is something like a *skill*, a skill which is required if one is to grasp religious truths.[2]

This book is shaped by two Kierkegaardian themes: 1. Faith is a trait of the whole person that is essential to gaining true religious knowledge; and 2. human reason has limits and it is reasonable to recognise those limits. The two themes are of course connected, in that faith provides the help that the limits of reason make necessary. My goal is to explore what is often called, pejoratively, fideism, so as to see what defensible insights can be gleaned from writers who have been called fideists. My goal is not to denigrate reason. Human reason surely has limits, and it hardly seems unreasonable to try to determine the nature of those limits.

In calling this book Kierkegaardian, I wish to acknowledge the great debt I owe to Kierkegaard. However, it will be obvious, I think, that there are many points where I disagree with Kierkegaard, and even more obvious, perhaps, that there are even more points where he would disagree with my book if he had the chance to read it.

I owe thanks to many living people as well. Kelly Clark and Merold

Westphal read through the entire work in draft form, and made many helpful suggestions. John Hare gave me help particularly on the Kant chapter, and Stephen Wykstra gave extra assistance on the chapter on the problem of evil. The entire Calvin philosophy department worked through two of the chapters in its departmental colloquium. Paul Helm also made many helpful suggestions on an earlier draft. Finally, Robert Huie prepared the bibliography of works cited, checked citations, and caught many mistakes by assisting in proof-reading the final typescript. Joel Schickel read page proofs and prepared the index. I am grateful to all of these people.

NOTES

1. *Søren Kierkegaard's Journals and Papers*, ed. and trans. by Howard V. and Edna H. Hong (Bloomington, Indiana: Indiana University Press, 1970) vol. II, pp. 13–14.
2. See *Journals and Papers*, vol. I, p. 5.

1

Introduction: The Problem of Faith and Reason

There is probably no word in the English language that is more complex and is used in more different senses than the word 'faith'. Religious faith is a concept that both friends and opponents of religion often misunderstand. Thus, the 'free-thinking' critic of religion alleges that religious belief is not backed up by evidence, but is held solely 'by faith'. The critic may mean by this simply that such beliefs have no support at all, but are something like a personal choice made for no good reasons. Embattled religious believers who have no answer for the sceptic may embrace the same impoverished view of faith, thus relieving themselves of any need to think about their beliefs.

Before beginning to look at religious faith, it is worth noting that the term 'faith' frequently has no special religious significance; in secular contexts we often talk of having faith *in* something or someone. For example, we speak of having faith in one's physician, faith in a political leader, faith in a research strategy in a scientific discipline, faith in a new drug used to treat a disease. Most broadly, and also closest to religious faith, would be the individual who has faith in a secular 'worldview' and/or a 'way of life' that might or might not be based on such a comprehensive vision of the world.

We also speak of faith *that* some event will occur or *that* some proposition is true. Thus I might say that I have faith that the economy will recover, or that the Republicans will win the next election. In this book we will mainly be interested in one special type of faith: religious faith. Nevertheless, it will sometimes be important as we consider religious faith to see its similarities and differences to what is called 'faith' in secular contexts.

In both secular and religious contexts, we sometimes speak of faith to highlight *uncertainty*. Thus, we might say, 'You don't really *know* that new policy will work as advertised; you just have faith that it will'. In this case to speak of faith is to emphasize the idea that a person cannot really be sure about something.

Paradoxically, we sometimes use the term in a way that connotes some kind of certitude, if not objective certainty: 'For Jim, it was an article of faith that the British parliamentary system was the best form of government'. Here an 'article of faith' seems to be something of which one is so certain that alternatives are not taken seriously.

In religious contexts the term 'faith' is often used more or less as a synonym for 'religion'. Thus, writers often talk about 'the Christian faith' and compare it to other 'living faiths', such as Islam or Hinduism.

Even more frequently the term 'faith' is used to describe a set of characteristics of the adherents of such a religion. But even here there is a bewildering complexity. When we speak of the faith of a Christian or a Hindu, some people wish to refer mainly to the *beliefs* of the individual, others focus on faith as *trust*, while others think of faith mainly as having to do with the *voluntary commitments* of the individual. Though these characteristics seem to be the major ones, other writers have focused on such qualities as psychological serenity, or have written about faith as closely related to such virtues as love and hope, or have thought of faith as some kind of all-encompassing attitude that colours the 'world' of the faithful person.[1]

This book is intended to explain and evaluate a particular view of the relationship of faith, particularly religious faith, to reason. With this limited focus, I cannot possibly survey all the various kinds of faith. Rather, what I must do is introduce one relatively clear concept of faith and talk about the relationship between faith in this sense and reason. Without some initial agreement on the meaning of 'faith' and 'reason' we cannot compare and evaluate rival accounts of their relationship.

It might, for example, turn out to be the case that apparently rival theories about the relation of faith to reason are not really rivals at all. If one person argues that faith must always be based on reason, and another person denies that, their argument may mask the fact that they mean different things by 'faith' or by 'reason'. This might occur, for example, if the individual who says faith must be based on 'reason' has a very broad concept of reason, including as 'rational' any belief that seems true to the individual, while the individual who says faith does not have to be based on reason regards as rational only beliefs that can be proved by logical argument. Similarly, two people may appear to agree on the relation between faith and reason, but the agreement may be superficial, hiding the fact that one person might think of faith as solely intellectual while the other might understand faith as entirely volitional in character.

So a certain amount of agreement in definitions is necessary to begin. Nevertheless, it is also important to define the concepts in such a way that genuine disagreements about the nature of faith and reason can occur. People can agree on a definition but still disagree about the nature of what is defined. As we shall see, in many cases disagreements about the relationship of faith to reason rest on such disagreements about the character of faith or reason, or both. In this chapter, I shall try to gain some clarity about the concept of faith, leaving the concept of reason for later discussion.

FAITH IN GOD

How then shall we think about faith? Because I know more about Christianity than other religions, and also because the relationship of faith to reason has been extensively discussed by Christians, I shall generally focus my discussion on Christianity and take most of my examples from the Christian tradition. The reader should, however, keep in mind that the philosophical problem of how faith relates to reason is one that applies to other religions, and even to secular 'faiths'.

In the great theistic world religions, notably Christianity, Judaism, and Islam, religious faith is closely tied to God. To speak of faith for a member of one of these religions is to speak primarily of faith in God. This of course does not solve our problem, but merely introduces a new concept. What is meant by 'God'?

Though of course there is diversity and much spirited disagreement about the nature of God among theologians, the great majority of religious believers think of God as a personal being who created and sustains the universe. God is thought of as all-powerful, all-knowing, and completely good, though there is not always complete agreement about what these terms mean. Most religious believers think of God as a spiritual being who has no bodily limitations and who in some sense transcends time, either by being everlasting or by being outside time altogether. To say God is personal in character is primarily to say that God is the kind of being with whom one can enjoy a personal relationship; though he is profoundly different from human persons in many ways, he is like them (or better, they are like him) in being intelligent (knowing truths, for example), in having intentions and in being able to carry out actions. In short God is capable of enjoying social relations with other persons. (Christians go on to believe that in being a Trinity, three persons in one, God's very being is social in character, even apart from his relations to humans and other persons.)

So what does it mean to have faith in such a God? Minimally, perhaps, it might mean *faith that God exists*. Certainly many discussions in the philosophy of religion focus on belief in God as a belief that there is a God. (The locution 'to believe in X' is ambiguous; it can mean just to believe that X exists, but can also mean that one believes that X is reliable, or that one trusts X.)

It is worth noting that faith in God, as it is understood in the Bible, is never understood merely as belief that God exists. Nor is this how most Christian theologians have thought of faith. The Bible never argues for or even asserts the existence of God. The Biblical narrative begins with the story of what God has done in creating the world, continues with God's dealings with a variety of people, leading to the calling of Abram out of Ur and the creation of a special people of God, Israel. In the Christian Bible, God's promises to Israel and interaction with his chosen people culminate in the coming of Jesus, the Anointed One, and the creation of the Church, a people of God not limited by ethnic or national boundaries. In this whole story, the existence of God is never argued for but simply presupposed.

It is true that the Bible shows some awareness of the fact that not everyone believes in God. Many people are regarded as worshipping false gods rather than the true God, and it is noted that the fool has said in his heart that there is no God (Psalm 14:1). In Romans 1, Paul explains that there is a natural knowledge of God, which is sufficient to make human beings responsible before God, but that this knowledge can be and has been suppressed. The Bible as a whole seems to assume that people are aware of God's reality, or at least that they can be aware of God without any special revelation or philosophical argument.

There certainly is such a thing as faith as belief that God exists, and there may be value in reflecting on how a person can obtain such a faith in today's world. We do not live in the same world as the people of Biblical times and what might properly be presupposed then may not be something that can be taken for granted today. Still, it is important to recognise that this kind of faith is not what is regarded as faith in the Bible, though it may turn out to be a component of Biblical faith.

BIBLICAL FAITH: TRUST, BELIEF AND OBEDIENCE

It has been claimed, rightly I believe, that the Biblical concept of faith includes three elements: trust, belief and obedience.[2] The most central element seems to me to be trust. The Biblical characters, such as Abraham,

Moses and David, who are held up as models of faith are first and foremost people who trusted God. I do not think that trust in a person, including trust in God, can be exhaustively analysed simply as belief in certain propositions, and so I agree with those who insist that Biblical faith is not merely belief that certain propositions are true.

However, it seems equally clear that faith includes or presupposes propositional belief, even if this is not all there is to it. Biblical faith shows itself primarily in believing what God has said. In the Biblical story, Abraham trusts God, and this is seen, among other ways, in his believing certain things because of what God has said to him. He believes, for example, that he will have a son and that through this son he will have many descendants, who will inherit the land to which God has led him and through whom all nations will be blessed.

Of course one does not usually believe what another person says without having some other beliefs about that person. Some philosophers actually argue that in order to have a reasonable belief in the testimony of another, we need evidence that this person's testimony is truthful, or that the person is reliable and truthful. This seems wrong to me, though the issue is controversial.[3] If I met a stranger and the stranger told me some important piece of information, I think it would be reasonable for me to believe the stranger, even if I had no positive evidence that the testimony was truthful or that the stranger was reliable. That is not to say, of course, that I should believe the stranger if I have some good reason to doubt the testimony. It is rather to embrace what is sometimes called 'the principle of credulity'. The principle of credulity says simply that it is reasonable to accept testimony as evidence unless one has reason to doubt the testimony. So if this principle is correct, I can accept a person's testimony without having other beliefs that serve as evidence for the truth of that testimony, and those philosophers who say that before believing testimony I ought first to have beliefs about the truthfulness of the content of the testimony or the reliability of the testifier are mistaken.

However, even if the principle of credulity is correct, and one needs no *evidence* to accept testimony, in the normal case a person will not believe what another person says without having some other beliefs about that person. Minimally, of course, one cannot trust a person unless one believes that person to exist. But this is pretty minimal. The principle of credulity only says that the fact that we have testimony in favor of a proposition gives us some reason to believe the proposition. This leaves open the possibility that in many cases we will also have reasons to doubt the proposition in question, and these cases will be numerous. In more doubtful cases, we are, quite properly, more likely to believe a person when we believe that person to be a person of good character. We are, for example, properly more likely to believe that a person will do what he or she promises when we believe that the promiser is a person who is trustworthy. To say that we *trust* a person is to say that one would be inclined to believe the person even when that person says something that one has some reason to doubt. Though trust can be present even where there is no reason to doubt, it shows itself particularly when there is reason to doubt. And in those cases we continue to believe, not just because of any general principle of credulity, but because we have certain convictions about the character of the person we trust. So trust in another person is linked to beliefs about that person in a double way; it seems not only to require that we believe what that person tells us, but to require that we do so partly because we have certain beliefs about the character of that person.

The final factor present in Biblical faith is that of obedience, a characteristic that is primarily moral.[4] The need for an additional factor is clear from the discussion of 'faith and works' in the Epistle of James in the New Testament. There the author argues that faith alone without works is 'barren'. He notes that though someone who believes in God 'does well', the demons have the same beliefs – and even the appropriate emotional response of trembling (James 2:19–20). Abraham was justified by works and not faith alone, according to the author. His claims here seem at least superficially in tension with the Apostle Paul's argument in Romans that salvation is through faith alone, and the writer of Hebrews 11, who cites the faith of Abraham and other heroes of the Old Testament as making them pleasing to God.

At the time of the Reformation there was an acrimonious dispute between Protestants and Catholics on the question of whether faith alone was sufficient for salvation or whether works were required as well. I believe that Richard Swinburne is correct when he maintains that this dispute was at least partly rooted in a verbal confusion.[5] The Catholic viewed faith as consisting merely of beliefs; in order for faith to be meritorious it needed to be joined with love, which includes a willingness to act in certain ways. By and large the Reformers had a different, larger conception of faith, one that saw it as necessarily linked with love and a corresponding willingness to act. Works were seen as the necessary fruit of faith, though they were not identified with faith, since that would suggest that salvation might be earned rather than being a free gift of God. No actual works are required for salvation. Nevertheless, faith was understood as a dispositional state, one of whose manifestations was a readiness to act obediently to God. It was not 'mere belief', of the sort the demons are said to possess, but in Swinburne's words, involved a readiness to act to achieve certain good purposes, 'relying on the belief . . . that God will do for us what we want or need'.[6]

So when Catholics insisted that faith alone (in the sense of mere propositional belief) was not sufficient for salvation, they were not necessarily contradicting the Protestant view that faith (in a richer sense that includes a willingness to be obedient) is sufficient. The Protestant concept of faith, while quite different from the Catholic concept of ordinary faith, is much more similar to what Aquinas called 'formed faith'.[7] Doubtless, some differences remain between the Catholic and Protestant positions, but the point is that there is some measure of agreement that the kind of faith that the Bible holds up as an ideal includes trust in God, beliefs about God and belief that what God has said is true, and a certain willingness to be obedient to God. These three components are not necessarily separable. Though we have seen that at least some of the beliefs that are ingredients in faith might exist apart from genuine faith, it is not always easy to distinguish trust, belief, and obedient action as distinct entities, for trust actually *consists* at least partly in having certain beliefs and in being willing to act in particular ways.

RATIONALISM: FAITH BASED ON REASON

Though it is clearly possible to act reasonably and unreasonably, and though we also sometimes speak of trust as unreasonable, it is mainly beliefs that have been the subject of reflection for philosophers who have focused on the reasonableness of religious faith. Even a cursory look at the history of Christian theology and philosophy shows that there have been strongly divergent approaches to the question of the relation between Christian belief and reason.

One approach, often labelled 'rationalism', claims that religious beliefs ought to be completely governed by reason. The rationalist perspective is perhaps most obvious in certain critics of religion. Twentieth-century philosopher Bertrand Russell, a notorious critic of Christianity, is reported to have been asked what he would say to God if, after death, he were to discover he had been wrong about religion, and found himself face to face with the deity. Russell is alleged to have responded that he would simply tell God 'not enough evidence'. Russell is typical of 'evidentialist' critics of religion, who think that religious belief would only be appropriate if it were based on sufficient evidence, and that no such evidence is available.[8]

It is important, however, to recognise that the rationalist claim that religious belief should be based on evidence is not merely made by opponents of religion who think that it cannot stand up to rational test, but by religious believers themselves who may be serenely confident in the rationality of their faith. This rationalist approach can be clearly seen in such thinkers as John Locke from the Enlightenment period, and Richard Swinburne in the twentieth century.[9]

Locke provides a specially clear example. He holds an 'evidentialist' ethic of belief, which enjoins that the degree of certainty of a belief should always be proportionate to the quality of the evidence. The basis for this requirement is 'the love of truth'. On the assumption that evidence is evidence of truth, he says that a person who loves truth must always exhibit the quality of not holding 'any Proposition with greater assurance than the Proofs it is built upon will warrant'.[10]

On Locke's view some religious truths are knowable by reason, which he defines as the ability the mind has to make discoveries and inferences based on the natural faculties of sensation and reflection.[11] Faith is understood as belief in a proposition 'upon the credit of the proposer, as coming from God' through a revelation.[12] Locke certainly thinks that human beings can by faith come to grasp truths they could not attain through natural human reason alone. Nevertheless, faith is still supported by and to some degree governed by reason.

One should never believe anything on the basis of a revelation that is contrary to what is known with certainty by reason, or in Locke's words, '*no Proposition can be received for Divine Revelation . . . if it be contradictory to our clear intuitive Knowledge*'.[13] Secondly, reason is given the task of determining whether an alleged revelation is genuinely from God. Though it is certain that whatever God has revealed is true, reason must judge whether any particular revelation truly comes from God, and a revelation should only be accepted if it has the backing of reason in this way.[14] By and large, then, for Locke revelation simply is 'natural *Reason* enlarged by a new set of Discoveries communicated by GOD immediately, which *Reason* vouches the Truth of', and so it is not surprising that he thinks there is no possibility of any inconsistency between faith and reason.[15] Locke is, however, willing to allow that a well-attested revelation might overrule what one holds by reason merely as a probable opinion or conjecture.[16]

FIDEISM: FAITH NOT BASED ON REASON

Though not all rationalists agree with the details of Locke's position, it is an excellent illustration of the general idea that faith must necessarily be governed by reason. The opposite view to rationalism is generally labeled *fideism* (from the Latin word for faith, literally 'faith-ism'). There are, as we shall see, many different views that are called fideism, but the root of the idea is that faith should not be governed or regulated by reason, where reason is understood to be an autonomous, relatively competent human faculty. The fideist says rather that faith must be accepted as at least partly autonomous or independent of reason, or even that reason must in some ways be corrected by or be made subservient to faith.

Why should someone take such a critical view of reason? If an individual cares about truth, and accepts Locke's view that reason is simply the means of attempting to reach truth, such a view would make no sense. Unsympathetic commentators on the fideistic perspective sometimes jump quickly to the conclusion that the fideist does not care about truth, but accepts religious beliefs because of some psychological motive such as fear or the need for comfort. However, such a conclusion seems to be not only uncharitable, but unsupported by evidence. For the fideist often claims to recommend faith precisely because it is the best way of obtaining the truth about religious matters.

In other words, the fideist typically rejects the rationalist assumption that reason is our best or even our only guide to truth, at least with respect to religious truth. The fideist sees human reason as limited, flawed, or damaged in some way. Thus, humans who rely on it to obtain religious truth will not achieve their end. For Christians the flaw is usually linked to the *sinfulness* of human beings. One of the central doctrines of Christianity is the claim that sin, understood as a rebellion against God, is a kind of spiritual disease that is endemic to humans. Fideists usually think that one of the baneful consequences of this illness is that human reason has been damaged in such a way that it cannot function properly so as to obtain the truth about God which humans need to have.

The idea that human reason may be corrupted by sin may appear strange, but a little reflection on some well-known facts of human psychology shows that the claim is by no means implausible. There are multitudes of examples of how human desires and emotions may affect the ways in which people interpret and weigh evidence. Suppose two individuals, one an ardent conservative and the other an ardent socialist, are watching a debate between two political candidates, who occupy opposite ends of the political spectrum. Both individuals watch the same debate; they have available to them exactly the same evidence. Yet one claims that the evidence clearly shows the conservative candidate won; the other enthusiastically maintains the opposite. What is happening? The two see the same evidence, but they do not see it in the same way because their own values shape the way they read that evidence.

Psychologists have discovered many ways in which human emotions and attitudes affect beliefs. A good illustration is the phenomenon of *cognitive dissonance*. Psychologist Leon Festinger developed this concept in an attempt to explain the behaviour of people who lived near but not in earthquake-prone areas. Festinger discovered a tendency for such people to spread unfounded rumours of disaster. He theorised that the people developed the beliefs in question because there was a tension between the feelings of anxiety they experienced and their actual situation of relative safety. In such a situation, in which there is a discrepancy between what our emotions suggest and the known facts, there is, he hypothesised, a tendency to reduce the tension by adjusting our beliefs to fit our emotions.[17]

This phenomenon is easy to understand because all of us have noticed such tendencies in ourselves from time to time. If we have engaged in an act that is morally dubious, which makes us feel guilty or uncomfortable, we are quick to invent new and more respectable descriptions and explanations for what we have done. Even our proverbs recognise the ways our emotions shape the beliefs we have about a situation. When we want what we do not possess, we say, 'The grass is always greener on the other side of the fence' to remind ourselves that our feelings may be falsifying the actual situation.

What bearing do such psychological facts have on the fideist claim that reason is damaged by sin? Insofar as sin is supposed to express itself in the desires and emotions of individuals, if reason is affected by those desires and emotions, then it is plausible that reason is affected by sin. We should be careful not to think that emotions always have a negative effect on reason; I shall later argue just the contrary. However, it is certainly true that emotions and desires can distort our rational faculties. If those emotions and desires are themselves distorted, which is at least part of what it means to claim that humans are sinful, then it is logical to think that our reason may be distorted as well. Furthermore, the claim that human emotions and desires are distorted or damaged is enormously plausible, given the tremendous amount of human selfishness and even wickedness portrayed on a regular basis on the nightly news, not to mention the selfishness most of us have found in our own experience and even – if we are honest – our own selves. So the fideistic claim that reason is damaged by sin is one that deserves to be taken seriously.

Sometimes this critical perspective on human reason expresses itself through opposition to *philosophy*, since philosophy is viewed as an expression of reason. Tertullian, for example, one of the fathers of the Church (c.160–230 AD), sees philosophy as the source of the errors introduced by various heresies into the Church. Tertullian believed that the truth about God has been given to humans by revelation, and that the surest way to truth is to rely on faith in that revelation, whose truth is grasped via humility and simplicity of heart. Hence he asks rhetorically, 'What indeed has Athens [the symbol of philosophical reasoning] to do with Jerusalem [the symbol of revelation]? What concord is there between the Academy and the Church? what between heretics and Christians?'[18]

Tertullian goes so far as to revel in the fact that the gospel appears absurd to philosophy; the death and resurrection of Jesus 'is by all means to be believed, because it is absurd . . . the fact is certain because it is impossible'.[19] It seems likely to me that Tertullian is not here saying that the gospel narrative is absurd or impossible to *him*. After all, he believes it to be true. Rather, he is probably best understood as saying that the fact that the gospel appears this way to natural human reason, shaped as it is by sinfulness, is an indirect mark of its truth.

Another Christian writer who is often cited in textbooks as a classic example of fideism is the nineteenth-century Danish thinker, Søren Kierkegaard. Kierkegaard was a very complex author who attributed many of his books to fictional characters who function as pseudonymous authors, and so we must be careful about attributing the views expressed in these books to Kierkegaard personally, as is often done by textbooks.[20] But regardless of whether or not the views expressed are Kierkegaard's personal statements, it is not hard to find statements in his writings that describe faith as something that is not supported by reason.

The pseudonymous 'author' of Kierkegaard's *Concluding Unscientific Postscript*, who is called Johannes Climacus, offers several reasons why religious faith, particularly Christian faith, should not be based on reason.[21] One argument given is termed by Robert Adams the 'approximation argument'. The idea here is that rational evidence for historical events (and Christian faith includes some such beliefs) can never be more than approximative. That is, the evidence for an historical belief can never establish that belief beyond any possibility of error.[22] However, according to Climacus, religious faith involves an 'infinite interest'. I think he means by this that the religious person's commitment to obtaining salvation is unlimited in character. For such an infinite interest, even small possibilities for error can be troubling. One might say there is an incommensurability between the desire of the individual for assurance and the evidence for truth that reason can offer. Not even the best scholars can overcome the gap between the 'quantitative character' of such evidence and the 'qualitative' character of the commitment that religious faith calls for: 'If all the angels united [to seek historical evidence], they would still be able to produce only an approximation, because in historical knowledge an approximation is the only certainty – but also too little on which to build an eternal happiness'.[23] I think this argument is better termed the 'incommensurability argument', because at bottom it rests on the contention that faith demands a kind of certainty that cannot be provided by reason. Faith and reason are incommensurable in the sense that they have no common measure that allows them to be joined together.

A second argument given in *Postscript* is called by Adams the 'postponement' argument. The ground of this argument is the claim that rational deliberation is in principle open-ended. No matter how much evidence one has, or how much time one has spent in considering that evidence, it is always possible that new evidence will appear, or that one would gain new insight from considering the available evidence again. The scholarly debate on such issues as the historical reliability of the New Testament, or with respect to philosophical arguments for the existence of God, has gone on now for hundreds of years and shows no signs of being concluded. If one attempts to base faith on such a process, then it would seem the decision as to whether to have faith must be postponed indefinitely. Or if the decision is not postponed, it must be a decision that is made only tentatively, subject to revision at any moment, which is the same as saying the decision cannot be made decisively. Yet Christian faith, according to Climacus, calls for just this kind of decisive commitment.

The third argument Adams terms the 'passion argument'. Here the idea is not merely that objective reasoning cannot provide the certainty that religious faith demands. Rather, the claim seems to be that genuine faith requires objective *uncertainty*, because faith demands risk. 'Without risk, no faith.'[24] Objective reasoning is thus criticised coming and going–for failing to attain certainty and for trying to do so. Genuine religious faith is a willingness to venture out 'over 70,000 fathoms of water'; it does not demand proof that one can swim before venturing into the water. Genuine Christian faith is faith in the incarnation of God in human form, something that appears to human reason to be 'the absolute paradox'.[25] Such a paradox is 'the absurd', and faith in the highest sense actually requires that its object be absurd. 'The almost probable, the probable, the to-a-high-degree and exceedingly probable – that he [the religious seeker] can almost know, or as good as know, to a higher degree and exceedingly almost *know* – but *believe* it, that cannot be done, for the absurd is precisely the object of faith and only that can be believed.'[26]

All these arguments against basing faith on reason seem to be rooted in an analysis of the concepts of faith and reason. However, I do not think these arguments are ultimately merely 'linguistic' in character. Rather, for Kierkegaard these conceptual points are rooted in the actual character of

Christian faith and human reason. The ultimate reason why reason and faith are seen as incommensurable is that human reason is distorted by sinfulness; from the point of view of Christian faith, human reason is 'untruth', and the Truth as well as the capacity to know the Truth must be given to human beings by God himself.[27] Christianity is concerned with how people can actualise Truth in their lives; it wants to see Truth not merely as propositions to be believed, but as something to be incorporated in the inner life, the 'subjectivity' of the individual.[28] However, the problem is that human subjectivity as it actually exists is untruth.[29] The person of faith thus finds it natural that human reason reacts negatively to faith. When reason blusters that the content of faith is absurd, the response of faith is essentially to say, 'Of course it looks that way to you; what else would you expect'.[30] The heart of what is called 'fideism' then lies in Christian claims about sin and the effects of sin on human reason.

If I am right in my contention that fideistic claims are closely linked to Christian views about sin and its effect on human reason, then fideism is of great importance for Christianity. Whether the position is ultimately defensible or not, it is at least rooted in concerns that lie at the very centre of Christianity. The critique of reason as affected by sin is by no means limited to thinkers like Tertullian and Kierkegaard. For this theme is quite central to major theologians such as Augustine, Luther, Calvin and Karl Barth. Of course some of these theologians are often characterised negatively as fideists, which often functions more as a term of abuse than a genuine descriptive term, but if the term does indeed fit such important thinkers of the Church, then fideism is a view that deserves thoughtful consideration.

CAN REASON BE SELF-CRITICAL?

As I have just hinted, fideism is often quickly dismissed as irrationalism. And it does seem that any rational defence of fideism will be difficult. If fideism is understood as an attack on reason, then it is hard to see how one can give rational arguments in favour of the view. It would seem one must at least tacitly assume the value of reason in order to use rational arguments at all. So how can one defend fideism?

Before defending or attacking fideism, we need to understand it better. I shall try in this book to show that fideism means very different things to different writers. Some views put forward under that label do indeed amount to irrationalism, and they turn out to be indefensible. However, I shall try to show that a good case can be made for some of the insights that lie behind the claims of thinkers like Calvin and Kierkegaard.

The central issue turns out to be the reasonableness of questioning the limits and competency of human reason. That human reason is limited in various ways is certainly not a controversial claim. Just about everyone recognises that human reasoning is finite–limited in many ways. So it can hardly be irrationalism to suggest that reason has limits, and that one should try to recognise those limits.

Whether a critique of reason amounts to irrationalism will depend on the nature of the critique. One problem of course is that if we say that it is reasonable to recognise the limits of reason, we are assuming that reason cannot be *completely* incompetent. For reason would have to possess a certain competence even to recognise where it is incompetent. No total rejection of reason can itself be argued to be reasonable, and any fideism that urges such a view deserves to be categorised as a form of irrationalism.

Ruling out irrationalism in this sense still leaves a wide field of investigation. After clearing the decks in the next chapter by examining and rejecting certain kinds of irrationalism, we shall proceed in the next several chapters to look at fideism as a way of posing questions as to how reason can become self-critical. Fideism poses thoughtful challenges in several ways. First we will look at the claim that religious truths can be known *without reasons*, or that religious beliefs do not have to be based on evidence. Next, we will look at the claim that certain kinds of truths are *above* reason, and hence not within the jurisdiction of reason. Finally, we will analyse the view that what might be called 'natural human reason' has some particular defects that make certain truths appear to go *against* reason, and that those truths can only be recognised by putting reason into question. I shall try to show that properly restricted versions of all of these fideistic claims are defensible. After examining such a 'responsible fideism' in general terms, I shall then try to make the discussion more concrete in the concluding chapters by looking at the implications of a fideistic view of faith and reason for such issues as how the knowledge that God exists can be attained, how the religious believer can reconcile faith in an all-powerful, completely good God with the existence of evil and suffering, as well as how distinctive doctrines of a particular religion, such as the Christian doctrine of the incarnation, can be known to be true.

NOTES

1. For a fine exploration of the complexities of the concept of faith see William Lad Sessions, *The Concept of Faith: A Philosophical Investigation* (Ithaca, New York: Cornell University Press, 1994). Sessions does not think the diversity of faith can be captured by a single concept, but regards the concept of faith as an 'analogical concept' in which there is no single 'essence' but where we can discern a number of overlapping 'family resemblances'. Sessions develops six 'models' of faith, each of which highlights a different feature. These are the Personal Relationship Model, the Belief Model, the Attitude Model, the Confidence Model, the Devotion Model (devotion to a way of life),

and the Hope Model. See p. 9 of his book for a chart summarising these different models.

2. Dewey Hoitenga, *Faith and Reason from Plato to Plantinga: An Introduction to Reformed Epistemology* (Albany, New York: SUNY Press, 1991) p. 38.
3. See C. A. J. Coady, *Testimony* (Oxford: Oxford University Press, 1992) for an excellent treatment of the problem of whether or not testimony needs evidential support in order to be rationally accepted.
4. Hoitenga, p. 38.
5. See Richard Swinburne, *Faith and Reason* (Oxford: Oxford University Press, 1981) pp. 104–24, particularly p. 114.
6. Swinburne, *Faith and Reason*, p. 118.
7. See Swinburne's discussion of Aquinas on this point in *Faith and Reason*, pp. 108–9.
8. A good example of a contemporary 'evidentialist' critic of religious belief, particularly Christianity, is Michael Martin, *The Case Against Christianity* (Philadelphia: Temple University Press, 1991). I discuss two kinds of evidentialism and present fideistic alternatives below in Chapter 3.
9. Richard Swinburne has written a whole series of books that defend the rationality of Christian faith, but his views on the question of how beliefs are to be based on evidence are most clearly presented in *Faith and Reason* (Oxford: Oxford University Press, 1981).
10. John Locke, *An Essay Concerning Human Understanding*, ed. Peter H. Nidditch (Oxford: Oxford University Press, 1975) Bk IV, Chp. 19, p. 697.
11. Locke, Bk IV, Chp. 18, p. 689.
12. Locke, ibid.
13. Locke, Bk IV, Chp. 18, p. 692 (emphasis Locke's).
14. Locke, Bk IV, Chp. 18, p. 695.
15. Locke, Bk IV, Chp. 19, p. 698.
16. Locke, Bk IV, Chp. 18, pp. 694–6.
17. For a clear explanation of cognitive dissonance, see David G. Myers, *Psychology*, 2nd edn (New York: Worth Publishers, 1988) p. 561.
18. Tertullian, *On Prescription Against Heretics*, in *The Ante-Nicene Fathers*, eds Alexander Roberts and James Donaldson, vol. III (Grand Rapids, Michigan: Wm B. Eerdmans, 1951) Chp. 7, p. 246.
19. Tertullian, *On the Flesh of Christ*, in *The Ante-Nicene Fathers*, p. 525.
20. For more on Kierkegaard and his relation to his pseudonyms, see my *Kierkegaard's* Fragments *and* Postscript*: The Religious Philosophy of Johannes Climacus* (Atlantic Highlands, New Jersey: Humanities Press, 1983) Chp. 1–3; and also my *Passionate Reason: Making Sense of Kierkegaard's* Philosophical Fragments (Bloomington, Indiana: Indiana University Press, 1992) Chp. 1.
21. These arguments are nicely explained, as well as criticised, by Robert Adams in 'Kierkegaard's Arguments Against Objective Reasoning in Religion', in his *The Virtue of Faith and Other Essays* (Oxford: Oxford University Press, 1987). I give a critical discussion of Adams' arguments in Chp. 7 below, pp. 106–10.
22. Søren Kierkegaard, *Concluding Unscientific Postscript*, trans. Howard V. and Edna H. Hong (Princeton: Princeton University Press, 1992) pp. 28–30. See also the 'Interlude' Section of Kierkegaard's *Philosophical Fragments*, trans. Howard V. and Edna H. Hong (Princeton: Princeton University Press, 1985) pp. 79–86.
23. Kierkegaard, *Concluding Unscientific Postscript*, p. 30.
24. Kierkegaard, *Concluding Unscientific Postscript*, p. 204.
25. Kierkegaard, *Concluding Unscientific Postscript*, pp. 580-1.
26. Kierkegaard, *Concluding Unscientific Postscript*, p. 211.
27. This is the central message of Kierkegaard's *Philosophical Fragments*. See pp. 13–20.
28. This is the meaning of the famous claim that 'truth is subjectivity'. See *Concluding Unscientific Postscript*, pp. 193–207.
29. Kierkegaard, *Concluding Unscientific Postscript*, pp. 207–11.
30. See the Appendix to Chapter III in *Philosophical Fragments*, pp. 49–54.

2

Fideism as Irrationalism

Fideism is, as we have already seen, not one view but a cluster of different claims. Terence Penelhum, in a valuable book *God and Skepticism*, makes a helpful distinction between what he calls 'evangelical fideism' and 'conformist fideism'. Penelhum understands fideism as primarily a religious or theological doctrine, one bound up, as I have claimed, with the thesis that human sin has so damaged human reason as to make it impossible for reason to evaluate religious truth claims properly.[1] Although this is a theological claim, Penelhum convincingly argues that philosophical doctrines may be urged in support of it. Specifically, fideists have often appealed to sceptical epistemologies to deflate the pretensions of reason. The arguments of sceptical philosophers purport to show that even beliefs about ordinary objects cannot be given rational justification. In light of this deficiency, reason should not presume to pronounce on transcendent matters.

As Penelhum describes the types of fideism, both 'conformist' and 'evangelical' fideists make this appeal to scepticism. The conformist fideist, however, is very different from the evangelical in that the conformist takes scepticism to entail that disputed religious questions really cannot be settled. The recommended solution is to 'conform' to the prevailing religious lifestyle and beliefs of one's environment without really embracing such beliefs in a wholehearted way. Penelhum discusses Catholic thinkers such as Erasmus, Montaigne and Bayle as examples of conformist fideism. These thinkers are interpreted as understanding religious faith as much more closely linked to conduct than belief. By embracing scepticism interminable doctrinal controversies are undermined and a simple, non-sectarian piety that centres on the practice of one's faith can be put forward. Such an attitude is similar to that recommended by some contemporary religious 'pluralists'.[3] Conformist fideism is suspicious, or indifferent to, campaigns to convert or evangelise people of other faiths.

Penelhum himself does not think that scepticism can be easily merged with true religious faith, and his concerns on this score are echoed by the other type of fideism he discusses, evangelical fideism. To the evangelical fideist, the faith of the conformist is really not faith at all, because genuine faith involves passionate commitments that are quite alien to the indifference of the sceptic. Yet the evangelical fideist has uses for philosophical scepticism as well. The evangelical fideist wishes to limit reason because it is believed that when reason is set aside, faith provides a way of grasping ultimate truth which is certain and definite. Such a stance fits much better with a sense that one's faith should be vigorously promoted to others, because the evangelical fideist is convinced that through faith one can find *truth*. The evangelical fideist often regards the conformist fideist with suspicion. As the evangelical fideist sees things, the conformist lacks true faith altogether. The evangelical fideist sees faith as including a conviction of the truth of certain beliefs, but a mere willingness to 'accept' the prevailing religious beliefs of a culture seems very different from such an assurance. The faith of the evangelical fideist seems more full-blooded and robust than that of the conformist fideist and thus in several ways more interesting. It is this type of fideism that will be my primary concern in this book, though later in this chapter I shall give some consideration to the other type of fideism.

I first want to examine some common and popular claims about the supremacy or autonomy of faith over against reason. I shall argue that these particular claims are irrational and indefensible, at least when they are read in what seems to be a straightforward, natural way. Though I shall illustrate these claims from the writings of various theologians and philosophers, it is the claims themselves in which I am interested. I do not claim that these views represent the last or best word of the writers from whom they are taken. Scholars may well argue that some of these quotations are taken out of context and do not really represent the final positions of the thinkers they are taken from. If so, I will be happy, because I have no desire to attribute unreasonable convictions to theologians or philosophers. Nevertheless, the ideas I shall discuss are quite important. Whether held by eminent theologians or not, I can testify from experience that they are held by many ordinary people.

The root idea behind the versions of fideism I regard as irrational is that genuine religious faith is *autonomous* in the sense of being exempt from rational, critical scrutiny. Sometimes this claim of autonomy is combined with polemical attacks on the competence of reason or assertions that faith and reason are locked in a battle in which reason must surrender. In this chapter, this claim of autonomy will be examined primarily with respect to the attitude of reason towards religious *beliefs*.[4]

Religiously, claims of autonomy of the 'evangelical' type are usually linked to the characteristic fideistic emphasis on the damaging effects of sin on human reason and the need for divine revelation. However, as Penelhum has urged, such claims of autonomy have been given philosophical justification by appeals to general philosophical claims about reason or rationality, and about language and meaning.

I shall distinguish three different forms of the autonomy claim, though in practice it is not always easy to determine which of these claims an author may be making, since it is arguable that the different forms are logically related in various ways. However, I think it is still useful to distinguish the following theses: 1. Human reason cannot legitimately examine or decide questions of religious truth at all. 2. The rational standards that must be used to determine questions about religious truth are internal to the religious life itself; religious beliefs cannot legitimately be examined by 'external' rational criteria of a general nature. 3. Religious commitments do not have objective, cognitive content; they are not answers to the kinds of questions that can be settled by objective reasoning at all, and so objective reasoning can neither support nor undermine such commitments.

CAN REASON EXAMINE RELIGIOUS BELIEFS?

Perhaps the boldest fideistic view is the blanket claim that human reason simply has no competence to deal with religious beliefs at all. Such an assertion is sometimes grounded in sweeping claims about the incompetence of reason as a whole. One way of trying to justify such a sweeping claim is to appeal to what might be called the 'no neutrality' thesis.[5] According to this thesis, though human reason would like to pose as a disinterested judge, it is never really objective. Rather, human beings are created by God and are held responsible to God by God. A human being who is not in a relationship of faithful obedience to the Creator is in a condition of rebelliousness, and this rebelliousness colours the whole of a person's being, including reason.

This no neutrality thesis is, as we shall see, very commonly held by fideists. Ultimately, I do not think that it can justify a blanket rejection of reason, but it certainly implies the possibility that reason is severely damaged and limited.

Cornelius Van Til, a twentieth-century Reformed theologian, sees 'unregenerated' human beings as rebellious creatures in this way. He argues that this condition not only makes it impossible for them to reach religious truths; it makes it impossible for them to reach truth of any kind. Though the grace of God does restrain the effects of sin, and rebellious humans never completely follow out the logic of their position, Van Til holds that rebellious humans are logically committed to 'presuppositions' that make it impossible for them to discover genuine truth. Hence, what might be called 'natural' human beings simply have no 'ability or right to judge of what is true or false, right or wrong'.[6]

Van Til therefore vigorously rejects the claim that apologetic arguments can be mounted that appeal to facts or logical principles that the unregenerate mind can grasp. Such an apologetic argument ignores the non-neutrality of human reason and implicitly concedes that sinful human reason can operate reliably. Van Til argues, for example, that one should not try to give rational arguments that the Bible is the inspired word of God. Rather, reason must begin with the presupposition that the Bible is the true word of God before it can even function properly: 'So we cannot subject the authoritative pronouncement of Scripture about reality to the scrutiny of reason because it is reason itself that learns of its proper function from Scripture'.[7] A human being must recognise that he is not autonomous, and in light of this learn to 'subordinate his reason to the Scriptures and seek in the light of it to interpret his experience'.[8]

One might wonder if Van Til has thereby made it impossible for Christians to defend their faith to non-Christians. It appears that there is no point of contact or common ground upon which an appeal might be made. Van Til's response to this is that the non-Christian really does know the truth and hence has the ability to recognise it when it is proclaimed and defended. The trouble is that non-Christians constantly suppress this knowledge because of their sinfulness. How can this suppression of the truth be overcome and the non-Christian brought to recognise the truth? Van Til says clearly that God must 'force an entrance'. 'As to the possibility and likelihood of the sinner's accepting the Christian position, it must be said that this is a matter of the grace of God'.[9]

What exactly does it mean to maintain that human reason has no competence to pronounce on religious matters? Van Til himself is none too clear about this question. Some theologians have maintained that logic itself, at least as we humans understand it, cannot be applied to God. Thomas Torrance, a disciple of Karl Barth, appears to suggest that this is so in some passages.[10] Our logic, he suggests, is somehow *ours* and we must not use it to try to confine God, who transcends all human thinking:

'Thus we must respect the importance and indeed the necessity of formal logic, but we cannot allow it to usurp the authoritative place occupied by the Truth Himself . . .'[11] Our logic is a 'paper-logic' and the God who is Truth cannot 'be domesticated and tamed and put into the strait-jacket of grammar and logic'.[12]

Russian expatriate Lev Shestov also suggests in his writings that faith does not accept the principles of logic as valid. Contrary to many religious philosophers who have thought that such logical rules as the principle of non-contradiction are necessarily true, Shestov asks rhetorically, 'From where does the Judaeo-Christian philosophy draw this unshakable conviction that the principle of contradiction cannot be overcome? Not from the Bible, surely'?[13] Shestov, in a manner similar to Torrance, does not seem to doubt the validity of logic because of the doctrine of sin, but rather because of a fear that allowing logical principles to be absolutely true would compromise the absoluteness of God.

This kind of thought is often expressed by those who reject reason's competence. The idea behind this worry seems to be that allowing reason critically to examine religious beliefs is somehow to make reason superior or even supreme and thus to make it into a kind of idol. So, for example, the theologian Karl Barth says that to reason about faith is to assume the standpoint of unbelief by making reason a kind of judge over Christ. Knowledge gained by reason implies the superiority of the knower to what is known. Barth says in contrast that 'knowledge of God . . . does not therefore permit the man who knows . . . to maintain an independent and secure position over against God so that from this he may form thoughts about God which are in varying degrees true'.[14]

It is difficult to see how the suggestion that the principles of logic are not valid or binding for faith can be accepted. People who make such suggestions usually think that religious truths are given to humans by a revelation that must be accepted through faith. But whether that revelation be thought of as consisting in events, or in events along with an inspired record, or exclusively in an inspired book, whatever truth is conveyed must surely be *understood* to be accepted.

This may not seem to be right, because in one sense of 'understanding' propositions held by faith may not be understood. This is the sense of understanding in which 'to understand' is to *see the truth* of the proposition. In this sense of the word, 'understanding' is something that faith seeks, but may not possess. To use a non-religious example, I may believe in the truth of Einstein's general theory of relativity without really understanding it.

However, there is another sense of understanding, where understanding is equivalent to grasping some kind of sense. Here understanding is not equivalent to seeing the truth of a proposition, but rather is a recognition of the sense of a proposition, or at least enough of that sense to determine that this is a meaningful proposition and not a string of meaningless sounds.[15] (Both kinds of understanding come, I think, in degrees.) Without understanding in this second sense, there can be no faith involving belief because there is nothing apprehended that could be the object of belief. If someone says to me 'gak ook mah' I cannot accept what the person says by faith. I do not even know whether or not the person has said anything at all. This second kind of understanding is one that requires the validity of principles of logic, because such principles make possible the recognition of the sense of a proposition and are the precondition of a proposition making sense. Logical principles such as those of identity and non-contradiction are presupposed in any attempt to grasp the meaning of a propositional revelation. If, for example, it is revealed that God calls human beings to believe that Jesus of Nazareth died for the sins of the world, then it must be presupposed that *this* is what is revealed; it is not revealed that Jesus did *not* die for the sins of the world. If one denied a principle such as the principle of identity (A = A) or the principle of non-contradiction (it is not possible for A and not-A both to be true), then it is impossible to make any sense of such a revelation. Any proposition revealed would be indistinguishable from its denial. It is for that reason that Kierkegaard, who is sometimes mistakenly thought to have endorsed the idea that religious

beliefs could go against logic, vigorously defended traditional Aristotelian logic over against its nineteenth-century Hegelian critics, even quoting (rather loosely and humorously) from *King Lear*. As Kierkegaard rephrases Shakespeare, faith calls that kind of reason that says 'yes and no to the same thing' a 'blockhead and a dunce'. Such reasoning 'is not good theology'.[16]

One might suppose that a revelation could overturn logic by revealing contradictory truths, thereby revealing that the principle of non-contradiction does not hold absolutely. However, reflection will show that this suggestion will not do.

It is true that religious believers sometimes hold *apparently* contradictory beliefs. And of course, it is doubtless true that religious believers, like everyone else, sometimes hold beliefs that are really contradictory. However, the believer does not accept that these beliefs are *in fact* contradictory. Take, for example, the beliefs that God controls all events and yet that human persons sometimes make free choices for which they are responsible. Such beliefs may appear contradictory, even to the believer. Nevertheless, the believer who accepts both beliefs cannot believe they are really contradictory, even if he or she does not know how they are to be reconciled. Believers cannot, for example, believe that accepting human freedom amounts to accepting God's lack of control, so that they both believe that God controls all events and at the same time believe that God does not control all events. If they do hold a belief like this one that appears straightforwardly contradictory, they will very likely hold that there is some respect in which God controls all events and some respect in which God does not. They cannot clear-headedly believe that God both does and does not control all events in exactly the same sense. For if both of these things are true, then what could it mean to affirm either that God does or does not control all events? So I conclude that the idea that faith requires or allows the rejection of basic formal logical principles cannot be a serious option.

Could faith require the rejection of reason in some broader sense of 'reason'? This question cannot be answered without some clarification of what is meant by 'reason'. As I see it, the term 'reason' is used in two fundamentally different ways. The concept of reason is partly a *normative* concept; it represents an ideal: the ideal of a set of processes that are aimed at truth and that give us the best shot of gaining truth. As a normative ideal the concept of reason can potentially serve to criticise any actual, concrete human thinking. We must be open to the possibility that our current ways of thinking and inquiring are not in fact truth-conducive.

However, the concept of reason must have some descriptive content as well; it cannot be purely normative without becoming purely abstract and irrelevant to our actual thinking. We do identify some of our ways of thinking as exemplifying those normative ideals and we hold those ways of thinking up as a measure of thought and inquiry.

Now it seems to me that the idea of rejecting reason in the purely normative sense makes no sense, unless one does not care about truth. By definition, reason in the normative sense represents whatever patterns or methods of thinking give us our best shot at truth; to reject reason in this sense is simply to indicate a lack of concern for truth.

However, it is by no means absurd to question whether particular patterns of thinking that are currently accepted as exemplifying this normative ideal in fact do so. For example, suppose someone identifies as 'rational' only those beliefs that can be verified by scientific evidence. To question the competence of 'reason' in this narrow sense is not to reject reason as an ideal; it can be convincingly argued that this restrictive view of reason is itself unreasonable, since obtaining scientific evidence itself seems to presuppose some beliefs that cannot be based on scientific evidence.[17]

We must be open then to the possibility that the patterns of thinking that are accepted as exemplifying the ideal of reason can be questioned. I shall try to show in succeeding chapters that this is a plausible way of understanding some of the claims of theologians about the limitations of reason.

However, it makes a great deal of difference how this criticism of what we might call 'concrete reason' is carried out. Some of the statements of theologians such as Van Til seem to suggest that the damaging effects of sin are such as to make it impossible for reason to understand its own limitations. On this view, the limitations of concrete reason are irremediable until that reason humbly submits to God and is miraculously transformed.

It is possible that such theologians are correct; at least I know no way of showing they are not correct. However, the stance they take has some major disadvantages. At the very least, one might say that the position adopted functions as a conversation-stopper. If I am told that my thinking is radically unsound, so unsound that it is not even possible for me to come to recognise the truth of the claim that it is unsound, there is little for me to say in return, since whatever I say will be dismissed as coming from a worthless source.

But the stance of the theologian who rejects reason as a whole is not only a barrier to dialogue. It is even a barrier to apologetic argument on the part of the theologian. If my reason is so totally flawed that I cannot recognise any truth, then it is pointless to present me with arguments or evidence for the truth of a view. As noted before, I cannot show that the theologian who takes such a standpoint is mistaken, and he may be willing to give up the enterprise of apologetics. But taking such a view seriously implies that one cannot, for example, give any reasons why one should have faith in Jesus of Nazareth rather than Mohammed (or vice versa) or accept the Bible as a revelation from God rather than the Koran (or vice versa). Once one has accepted the true revelation, the theologian may hold that one will be able to see the truth since reason will be healed. But it looks as if the acceptance of that true revelation will be rationally arbitrary.

There is a possible rejoinder to this argument that apologetic arguments are pointless for this kind of fideist. Theologians such as Van Til may hold that the choice of true faith is grounded in God's miraculous action. Perhaps this possibility makes the giving of apologetic arguments sensible, since the apologist can rely on the possibility of divine action to enable the hearer to respond. Although one cannot say that arguments in such a case would be necessary, since God could do the miraculous work in question apart from any argument, there is no reason why God could not make the arguments the occasion for his work.

Still, apart from positing this kind of miracle, from the point of view of what we might call a sincere seeker, the absolute claims of this kind of religious fideist are of little value. Such claims only serve to block any serious discussion of religious truth and make it impossible for the seeker to understand why faith should be extended to one alleged divine revelation in the face of a plurality of religions.

The remedy is not for concrete reason dogmatically to rule out the possibility that it needs criticism. As we shall see, there is a strong tendency for human beings to identify concrete reason with normative, ideal reason and treat any criticism of the former as a rejection of the latter. Such an attitude deserves critical examination. But no critical examination can be conducted if one assumes in advance that reason is so universally incompetent that it cannot even recognise the faults of such dogmatic attitudes.

LANGUAGE GAMES AND RELIGIOUS AUTONOMY

A second type of fideism, inspired by some of the writings of Ludwig Wittgenstein, does not necessarily reject the idea that religious beliefs can be rationally examined at all, but rather questions whether or not the standards of rationality that are appropriate for the task are *internal* to the life of religious faith itself rather than being external to it. Perhaps religious beliefs are not autonomous in the sense of being absolutely exempt from rational scrutiny, but are rather autonomous in the sense that the rational standards that must be employed are themselves part of the religious outlook. The general idea that underlies this seems to be that what counts as 'rational' must be determined by context; there is no such thing as rationality in general apart from specific human activities.

According to this view, the meaning of our concepts is derived from the role they play in specific 'forms of life', which are expressed in various 'language games'. Norman Malcolm, a follower of Wittgenstein, writes that both religion and chemistry can be seen as such language games. Both are 'systems of thought and action' where there are 'advances and recessions of insight'. Within such a system of thought there are rules for what is to count as evidence and what is to count as a mistake; particular beliefs can be shown to be justified or unjustified.

However, according to Malcolm, following the lead of Wittgenstein, eventually such justification comes to an end. At some point, we simply say that 'this is what we do', or that 'this language game is played'. There can be no justification for the language game itself, or the 'framework principles' that are its constitutive foundation.[19] As an example of this, Malcolm cites our unquestioning assumption that physical objects do not just vanish into thin air or go out of existence without some physical explanation. When we lose an object, we search for it and never take seriously the possibility that the object has just ceased to be, with no physical cause of its destruction such as being blown up. We can imagine a society in which such a possibility is taken seriously, and where people believe that on rare occasions, objects just do vanish in this way. Malcolm argues that we have no real evidence that this is not so; we embrace our own way of thinking because it is simply part of the framework of our thinking about physical objects, a basic foundation of what might be called the physical object language game.

This belief in the permanence of physical objects does not have the status of an hypothesis for us; we neither have nor require evidence for it. Malcolm argues that for some religious people, belief in God has the same kind of status. Such people do not regard their belief in God as an hypothesis for which evidence is required. Rather, it is a framework principle of the religious life. From within that way of life, some assertions about God can be seen to be reasonable or unreasonable, coherent or incoherent, but Malcolm argues that it makes no sense to try to evaluate such a way of life itself as a whole on the basis of supposedly objective standards of evidence that apply to all beliefs.

Critics of this view, which is often called 'Wittgensteinian fideism', have raised a number of acute problems.[20] First of all, there is a question as to whether religious 'forms of life' and their accompanying 'language games' are so insulated from other forms of life and language games as to be autonomous in the way Malcolm suggests. It would seem that religious ways of life and accompanying language games overlap considerably with such language games as the 'physical object language game' and the 'historical event language game'. Christian faith, for example, involves beliefs that God has created the physical world, and that people who die 'in Christ' will be raised from the dead as bodily beings. This would seem to imply that Christians hold that physical objects would not exist without God and that physical death is not necessarily the end of a person's physical existence.

When different language games overlap in this way, the possibility opens up that beliefs that are part of one language game may be confirmed or disconfirmed by beliefs that are not strictly internal to the language game. A person who affirms the Apostles' Creed, for example, one of the earlier statements of Christian belief, says that he believes that Jesus 'suffered under Pontius Pilate'. The point of this part of the creed seems to be to affirm that the passion narrative about the death of Jesus recounts actual historical events, events that occurred at a particular point in time. If these historical events did not occur, then it would seem that the person who affirms the creed is mistaken on at least some points. The truth or falsity of the creed is then partly a matter of what really happened.

Suppose someone came to believe on the basis of historical evidence that the creed was false on these points. It would hardly do in such a case to claim that this does not matter because the rules internal to the language game license an affirmation of the creed. It is unhelpful to be told that the people in a particular community regard it as legitimate to affirm these historical events if one thinks they did not in fact occur.

Historical events might be thought of as a special case that involves special problems, and of course there are Christians who wish to drop any historical belief and regard the founding narrative of their faith simply as a non-historical myth. However, essentially the same problem recurs with respect to belief in God. The religious person who believes in God believes that it is a fact that God exists: that an all-powerful, all-knowing, all-good person created the universe and sustains it. Many Christians believe that this God hears prayers and answers them, and that God is involved in human affairs and will ultimately bring history to a conclusion in which good will triumph over evil.

Someone who believes these things believes they are real facts. There are of course big questions over how a person might come to know such truths, but one cannot believe them to be true and at the same time hold that their objective truth is unimportant. Suppose, for example, that someone is convinced by philosophical argument that the concept of an all-powerful being is incoherent and thus that the assertion of the existence of such a being is self-contradictory. It will not do to reply that this does not matter because the rules of the religious language continue to affirm the reality of God. It is of little comfort to be told that a particular community talks as if God were a reality, if one thinks God cannot be a reality.

It is important to see that this belief in the objectivity of God's reality is not an external imposition on Christian faith. It is not, for example, a misplaced application of contemporary scientific criteria of rationality to religious questions. Rather, the assumption that truth is objective is the way faith itself thinks of the matter from the 'inside'.[21] Faith does not think that 'speaking (or thinking) makes it so', and its claim is not merely that God is a reality for the religious community but that God is the reality upon whom everything else depends.

Norman Malcolm argues that the religious person believes *in* God, but that no sense can be given to a belief in the existence of God.[22] His argument for this seems to be that 'belief in God does require . . . some religious action, some commitment, or if not, at least a bad conscience'.[23] But even if we agree with Malcolm here, this seems only to imply that a religious believer never has a mere belief in the existence in God, apart from a fuller and richer set of beliefs and attitudes. Malcolm seems to be saying that religious believers never have a 'bare' belief that God exists; rather they have a rich set of beliefs that are set in a rich religious life. However, this by no means implies that this richer set of beliefs does not include or presuppose a belief that God exists. Indeed, how could it not? I could hardly pray to a God whom I did not believe existed.

A closely related problem follows from this. Since language games are not autonomous and insulated, it is not true that language games as a whole cannot be rationally scrutinised. At least some of them can. Consider, for example, the case of astrology, which certainly appears to be a language game of its own. We surely cannot simply say that 'this language game is played' and ask no questions about its rationality. Someone who makes important decisions on the basis of astrology (as was claimed of a recent American president) can legitimately be asked such questions as the following: Are the predictions of astrology specific enough to be checked? Is there any plausible explanation of how the positions of stars could be linked to events in human life? If critical evaluation of astrology is possible, it is hard to see why the same might not be true of systems of religious belief. At least we would need some good reason to think that this is not possible for the case of religious belief systems.

There are important lessons to be learned from the Wittgensteinian fideist. One is that to understand religious beliefs we must understand them in their context, see how they appear 'from the inside' so to speak. Another is that questions may legitimately be asked about the appropriateness of the rational standards used to evaluate religious beliefs. It may well be the case that the Wittgensteinian is correct in asserting that sometimes religious beliefs are subjected to demands that are inappropriate and make no sense once those beliefs are understood in their context. It is true that religious assertions are not scientific assertions, for example, and so it may be unreasonable to demand that they satisfy scientific criteria of rationality. But these lessons do not imply that religious beliefs can be insulated from critical scrutiny of a general nature altogether.

RELIGIOUS ANTI-REALISM

The third kind of fideism that I wish to criticise in this chapter is the most radical view of all. To understand this kind of fideism, we should return to the Wittgensteinian fideist's position. In criticising the Wittgensteinian, I assumed a common-sense realism, in which to believe in God as creator of the universe is to believe that this is an objective truth. From the point of view of such a realism, if God truly exists and created the universe, then this is so regardless of whether any human being thinks that it is so, or even whether there are any human beings at all. Truth is independent of human beliefs. It is this common-sense realism that allowed me to criticise the view that religious beliefs are autonomous and insulated from criticism.[24]

One possible response to this criticism is to reject this implied realism. Suppose one rejects the idea that God is an objective reality regardless of whether humans acknowledge his reality. Suppose one rejects the whole notion that religious truth is independent of human beliefs and actions. From such a perspective, it would perhaps make some sense to hold that if a particular community thinks and speaks of God as a reality, then from the point of view of that community, God is a reality.

Some of the Wittgensteinian fideists who hold views similar to those of Malcolm seem at least to flirt with this way of construing religious beliefs. D. Z. Phillips, for example, has argued that prayer should not be understood as a literal conversation with God in which one might petition God to bring about particular events.[25] If one thinks of a petitionary prayer as an attempt at influencing the divine will 'one is back in the realm of superstition'.[26] Phillips thinks that such prayer is similar to a magical incantation, and argues that a genuinely religious petitionary prayer 'is best understood, not as an attempt at influencing the way things go, but as an expression of, and a request for, devotion to God through the way things go'.[27]

It is not clear to me that such a request for devotion is not a petition for God to bring about a certain state of affairs, namely the state of affairs in which the petitioner possesses a certain attitude of devotion. But perhaps Phillips would say that this attitude is achieved through ordinary psychological processes. The prayer may simply be a technique that is likely to result in the desired attitude, and hence no supernatural activity on God's part is required. Regardless of what he would say on this question, the general tendency of Phillips' treatment of prayer is to make the question of whether God truly hears prayer and answers it completely independent of any empirical question about what happens in the world.

In a similar manner, when writing about life after death Phillips claims that a religious faith in the immortality of the soul does not involve any factual claims about what may happen after death. Rather, to believe in life after death is to employ a certain 'picture', say of a final judgment, that one brings to bear on issues that face one in *this* life.[28] Imagine, Phillips says, a man who has a picture of his family being reunited after death: 'The picture of the family reunion after death is not a prediction for which he has evidence, but a vision in terms of which much of his own life is lived out. The picture is not assessed by appeal to evidence'.[29]

The 'truth' of such a picture, if one wishes to speak of truth in this connection, must lie in the quality and integrity of the life that the picture helps to make possible. Believing in pictures of life after death 'has to do with living by them, drawing sustenance from them, judging oneself in terms of them, being afraid of them, etc.'.[30]

Whether Phillips really wishes to extend this kind of non-cognitive analysis to the religious life as a whole is difficult to say. I do not know, for example, whether or not he would treat the question of God's existence as a matter where there is no objective truth of the matter. However, theologian Don Cupitt has developed this line of thought and explicitly embraces the idea that the religious life as a whole must be understood as non-cognitive and 'expressive' rather than being about objective realities.[31]

From Cupitt's point of view, talk of God is (or rather, should be seen as) a pictorial, projective way of talking about what he calls the 'religious requirement'. He believes that 'religious language is basically expressive in force, not descriptive. God's reality is not a matter of facts and evidence, but of the unconditional authority of religious categories in a person's life.'[32] From this point of view, my criticism of the Wittgensteinian fideist (that we cannot determine what is true by the way we talk) fails, for truth *is* ultimately determined by language, and the experience shaped by language:

> The expressivists . . . say that the sense in which mathematical objects like numbers 'exist' is given in the way mathematicians talk about numbers, and the sense in which physical objects like chairs exist is given in the way we talk about physical objects. Similarly, the sense in which God is real is given in the language and practice of religion.[33]

Of course, depending upon one's philosophy of mathematics and of physical objects, one might argue that even if our concepts of numbers and physical objects are shaped by the way we talk, the reality of numbers and physical objects is not dependent on human language. But Cupitt consistently reinterprets all religious language in an 'anti-realist' way. For example, he claims that prayer is really a way of trying to change oneself, a kind of meditation or a way of expressing how seriously we are committed to certain ideals.[34] When I confess God as creator I do not say anything about the dependence of the natural world on an infinite being; rather 'I testify to my experience of rebirth and renewal insofar as the religious concern and religious values really have come to take first place in my life'.[35]

This kind of non-cognitive account of religious belief of course eliminates any need for reason to consider religious truth claims, since no such claims are made, at least of a non-ethical or practical kind. As for the 'religious requirement' or the 'religious ideals' to which the religious person is committed, Cupitt does not see these as commitments that can be rationally scrutinised or justified either. His argument is that these values are fundamental to our sense of self; we have no higher standpoint from which they could be supported. Though there are clearly many religious perspectives, as well as non-religious ones, which could be embraced, there is no way to argue for the superiority of one over another:

> There are many forms of faith, each with an associated cluster of characteristic values and virtues; but since the decision of faith comes first – so much as to constitute the form of our personhood – it is hard to imagine oneself making a reflective choice between forms of faith from some standpoint anterior to any of them. So it is hard to see what could count as a justification of the fundamental religious commitment . . .[36]

This strand of Cupitt's thought seems similar to the view that is sometimes characterised as 'religious pluralism', a view that rejects any attempt to claim that religions can be compared and judged to be more or less true. If religions do not make truth claims at all then it seems obvious that one cannot be judged truer than another. If this is the way things are, then it makes little sense for people to convert to other religions because they have come to see their old faith as false or less true than some other one. Rather, the attitude of the person Penelhum calls the 'conformist fideist' would seem to be more appropriate, in which one chooses a religion on pragmatic grounds. For the most part, the conformist fideist recommends acceptance of the religion that is appropriate to one's own culture, or perhaps if there is some choice in one's culture, acceptance of the religion that fits one's own needs.

Cupitt seems correct in maintaining that if religious faith involves no beliefs about objective truths, then it does not require any critical scrutiny, though one might wonder whether ethical attitudes constitute 'radical choices' for which no justification can be given. However, I believe Cupitt is mistaken when he maintains that this expressivist account of religious faith does not lose anything of essential value.

Cupitt is candid and clear-headed in admitting that his account of faith differs from traditional views. He says, for example, that on his view, Christians should come to view what he calls traditional Christianity in much the same way as Cupitt thinks some traditional Christians view the Old Testament.[37] He recognises that traditional Christian faith did involve belief in a God who created the world, acted decisively in Jesus Christ to redeem a fallen world, and who will someday bring about his ultimate goal of a kingdom of righteousness. Cupitt claims that such traditional beliefs are no longer credible; in this respect Cupitt rejects fideism and says that certain religious beliefs are ruled out by reason. These claims of Cupitt that such traditional beliefs are no longer credible are of course hotly debated by contemporary philosophers of religion and I cannot settle the issues at this point.

I think the more important claim on the part of Cupitt is not that such beliefs are irrational; it is that they are religiously useless or even harmful. His argument here is rooted in the view that an authentic human life must be an *autonomous* one. Moral and spiritual ideals can only be truly moral and spiritual if they are ideals that are in an important sense *mine*, and Cupitt takes this to mean that I myself must be the source of their authority and validity. He believes that an objective God who stands over against the individual could have no relevance to the moral and spiritual life; only a God who is simply a projection of my own ideals can be a worthy 'God' for me.

Such an ideal of autonomy seems dubious to me. Cupitt seems to be confusing two distinct ways in which an ideal could be said to be mine. An ideal could be mine in the sense that I *constitute* or *create* the ideal. But an ideal could also be mine in the sense that *I* truly recognise the ideal as binding. It is undeniable that ideals must be internalised in the second sense, and therefore there is a sense in which moral and religious ideals presuppose the individual's autonomy. But it does not follow from this that I must be, or even can be, the source of the authority of the ideal.

It is somewhat ironical that Kierkegaard, whom Cupitt regards as a kind of hero, has a devastating critique of the kind of autonomy that Cupitt endorses. Kierkegaard calls this kind of autonomy 'the despair of defiance'. According to Kierkegaard, it is not true that the self is autonomous; we are thoroughly relational creatures, dependent for our sense of self on others, and ultimately on some 'power' that is the ground of the self. The autonomous self attempts to declare its independence and make itself this 'power'. The problem is that the ideals such a self recognises can really have no binding authority, for the choices of the self in such a case are arbitrary and groundless. An ideal can only really be binding if it is perceived that the ideal has some validity independently of the self:

> If the self in despair is an *acting self*, it constantly relates itself to itself only by way of experiments, no matter what it undertakes . . . It recognises no power over itself; therefore it fundamentally lacks earnestness, even when it gives its utmost attention to its experiments.[38]

Insofar as the self is conscious that its 'ideals' are arbitrary and groundless, it cannot take these ideals as truly binding:

> The self is its own master, absolutely its own master, so-called; and precisely this is the despair . . . On closer examination, however, it is easy to see that this absolute ruler is a king without a country, actually ruling over nothing; his position, his sovereignty, is subject to the dialectic that revolution is legitimate at any moment.[39]

I do not, as Cupitt thinks, 'choose my religion, all of it', because 'I impose the religious requirement upon myself'. Most truly religious people have a sense that their faith is something that in a sense chooses them. I cannot be absolutely committed to what Cupitt calls 'the pearl of great price' and at the same time think that the ideal that constitutes this pearl is merely a groundless choice.

What is the alternative to groundless choice? The idea of a groundless or 'radical' choice, a choice made for no reasons as the foundation of the ethical and spiritual life, has its roots in the conviction that the realm of facts is absolutely divorced from the realm of values. The realm of facts is the realm of truth; our attitudes and actions cannot be appropriate or inappropriate to this value-free reality. It is crucial to see that such a vision of reality is a metaphysical vision; it is equivalent to a kind of metaphysical materialism. In the end metaphysics cannot be avoided; questions about values are always grounded in convictions about what kind of a universe this is. The conviction that values are essentially arbitrary human choices rests on a metaphysical picture that sees values as having no standing in reality.

We can see from this that beliefs about the character of the universe and the place of human beings within it are not religiously idle. Classical attempts to justify a particular view of the good life and how it should be sought were generally grounded in some account of what human beings were really like, and what purposes and ends we have.[40] Such accounts cannot be divorced from accounts of the meaning of the universe of which humans are so evidently a part.

Cupitt seems to think of God very crudely as a kind of cosmic briber who would corrupt our moral lives by tempting us to do good for the sake of some crass, extrinsic reward. It never seems to have occurred to him that the goal of the moral and spiritual life might be *community*, communion with others committed to one's own flourishing as well as the flourishing of others, rather than autonomy, and that communion with a supremely good, loving person would be the highest conceivable form of this goal.

Certainly, if one thinks of religious faith as an arbitrary, unjustifiable choice as to how one should live, a choice that cannot be justified by any considerations about what human beings are really like or their place in the cosmos, then rational appraisal of religious belief will be pointless. However, it seems quite dubious that reflection on how human life should be lived can be divorced from questions about the character of reality itself. It does not seem that Cupitt himself has been able to divorce the two; rather his views on the character of the ethical life as a 'radical choice' seem to reflect a kind of naive scientific materialism, a faith that science tells us all the truths there are about the universe, which is of course a claim that science itself does not and cannot make.

So it does not seem surprising that religious people – Christians, Jews, Muslims, Hindus, even Buddhists – should continue to justify their allegiance to their moral and spiritual ideals by appeals to the character of reality. It is important to see that the question of God's reality is a question about the character of the whole of reality. God is not just 'one more thing'. If God exists, then there is a spiritual and moral purpose at the bottom of the whole of reality; if God does not exist then this is not the case. So most religious believers will continue to see their faith as linked to claims about the character of reality, and there is no reason why they should not do so. And insofar as they do make such claims, the question as to how their beliefs can be known or justified remains a pressing one.

Fideism as the blanket dismissal of rational reflection about religion seems unreasonable. Of course the fideist can always say that this does not matter to him, and if so, the conversation will come to an end. But most people do care about truth. Insofar as 'reason' is understood normatively as a way of getting at truth, whatever that may be, most people will be open to thinking about their beliefs.

NOTES

1. Terence Penelhum, *God and Skepticism* (Dordrecht: D. Reidel Publishing Co., 1983) p. 1.
2. See Penelhum, pp. 18–39.
3. The inverted commas here are to indicate that the term 'pluralist' is a contested one. Some thinkers claim that pluralism does not allow for particular religions making any claims of superiority over others with respect to claims of truth. Such a view in my opinion is not genuinely pluralistic in that it does not respect the differences between religions but imperialistically legislates what a religion may or may not do.
4. Though it should be kept in mind that faith is not merely propositional belief. The notion of faith as trust will become important in later chapters.
5. Although the roots of this view can be traced back through Calvin to Augustine and the New Testament, one of its most influential advocates was the Dutch theologian and political leader Abraham Kuyper. Though Kuyper was an influential advocate of the 'no neutrality' thesis as I have described it, he qualified this thesis with a view of God's common grace, and also with a qualification that in areas of life outside of morals and religion, areas that are outside the 'spiritual sciences', the lack of neutrality has less impact and may for some purposes be thus ignored. Kuyper thus accounts for the fact that the non-Christian can 'weigh and measure' accurately and so do

science together with Christians. Thus I do not think Kuyper would accept some of the views discussed in this chapter. See his *Encyclopedia*, Vol. II, pp. 95–8 cited in Cornelius Van Til, *The Defense of the Faith*, 3rd edn (Phillipsburg, New Jersey. Presbyterian and Reformed Publishing Co. 1955) pp. 286–90.

6. Van Til, p. 212.
7. Van Til, p. 108.
8. Ibid.
9. Van Til, p. 149.
10. See Thomas F. Torrance, *Theological Science* (London: Oxford University Press, 1969) pp. 54, 153, 205 and other passages.
11. Torrance, p. 219.
12. Ibid.
13. Lev Shestov, *Athens and Jerusalem* (Athens, Ohio: Ohio University Press, 1966) p. 302.
14. Karl Barth, *The Knowledge of God and the Service of God According to the Teaching of the Reformation* (New York: Charles Scribner's Sons, 1939) p. 104.
15. Thomas Aquinas seems to speak of both of these senses of 'understanding'. He says that when 'understanding' is taken in the sense that implies 'apprehending the essence of the understood thing' then faith is incompatible with understanding in *Summa Theologiae*, 2–2, Q. 8, A. 2, p. 153. Cited from *On Faith: Readings in the Summa Theologiae*, trans. Mark D. Jordan (Notre Dame, Indiana: University of Notre Dame Press, 1990). However, he also says that 'faith cannot universally precede understanding; for man cannot assent to some proposed things through believing unless he understands them somewhat' (2–2, Q. 8, A. 8, p. 167). All references to ST 2–2 will be taken from the Jordan translation cited here.
16. Søren Kierkegaard, *Philosophical Fragments* (Princeton: Princeton University Press, 1985) p. 53.
17. For a clear discussion of this point and argument that science presupposes truths that are not themselves truths of science, see Del Ratzsch, *Philosophy of Science: The Natural Sciences in Christian Perspective* (Downers Grove, Illinois: InterVarsity Press, 1986) pp. 97–8.
18. Norman Malcolm, 'The Groundlessness of Belief', in Louis Pojman, *Philosophy of Religion*, 2nd edn (Belmont, California: Wadsworth, 1994) p. 466.
19. Malcolm, p. 463.
20. See, for example, Michael Martin's discussion in *Atheism: A Philosophical Justification* (Philadelphia: Temple University Press, 1990), and Kai Nielson, *An Introduction to the Philosophy of Religion* (New York: St Martin's Press, 1982).
21. By 'objectivity' here I mean simply that God's reality is not dependent on human beliefs or emotions.
22. Malcolm, p. 468.
23. Ibid.
24. The common-sense realism which I discuss and defend here should not be identified with various metaphysical theories that may incorporate but also go beyond common sense on this point. Nor should the denial of my common realism be identified with the denial of those more embellished metaphysical theories. Philosopher Merold Westphal, for example, defends a view that he calls 'anti-realism' but one that allows for truth, including religious truth, to be at least relatively independent of us humans, so that whether or not God is real does not depend on the affirmation of a religious community. Westphal's 'anti-realism' is thus a form of common-sense realism in my sense. See his 'Christian Philosophers and the Copernican Revolution', in *Christian Perspectives on Religious Knowledge*, ed. C. Stephen Evans and Merold Westphal (Grand Rapids, Michigan: Wm B. Eerdmans Publishing Co., 1993) pp. 161–79.
25. D. Z. Phillips, *The Concept of Prayer* (London: Routledge and Kegan Paul, 1965).
26. Phillips, p. 120.
27. Phillips, pp. 120–1.
28. D. Z. Phillips, *Death and Immortality* (London: MacMillan, 1970), pp. 64–70.
29. Phillips, *Death and Immortality*, pp. 68–9.
30. Phillips, *Death and Immortality*, p. 68.
31. Don Cupitt, *Taking Leave of God* (New York: Crossroad, 1981).
32. Cupitt, p. 56.
33. Cupitt, p. 57.
34. Cupitt, pp. 128–36.
35. Cupitt, p. 55.
36. Cupitt, p. 120.

37. I think Cupitt does not properly understand the way traditional Christians in fact view the Old Testament.
38. Søren Kierkegaard, *The Sickness Unto Death* (Princeton: Princeton University Press, 1980) p. 68. I have modified the translation.
39. Kierkegaard, *Sickness Unto Death*, p. 69. (translation modified).
40. For a good discussion of the history of attempts to ground values in the nature of reality, see Arthur Holmes, *Fact, Value, and God* (Grand Rapids, Michigan: Wm B. Eerdmans, 1997).

3

Faith Without Reasons: Is Faith Based on Evidence?

The claim that religious faith is completely autonomous and immune from rational scrutiny cannot itself pass rational scrutiny. Or so I have argued in the last chapter. However, there are a number of other claims in the neighbourhood of fideism that have much more plausibility. In the remainder of the book I shall examine a number of these suggestions, including the claims that faith is legitimate *without* reasons, that it is in some sense *above* reason, and finally that it may in some respects properly go *against* reason. In this chapter I shall examine the idea of faith as believing without reasons.

EVIDENCE, BASIC BELIEFS, AND THE ETHICS OF BELIEF

What might it mean to believe without reasons? If we take 'reasons' very broadly this is probably not possible. The term 'reason' can refer both to a cause (as in 'the reason that event happened') and also a motive (as in 'the reason he committed the crime'). Beliefs, along with just about everything else about humans, presumably have causes, and to the degree that they are voluntary actions, they doubtless are motivated by reasons. However, the term 'reason' can also refer to *evidence*, as in 'you have no reason to believe that claim'. Some philosophers have claimed that it is possible to hold a belief that is not based on evidence, and so if by a reason for a belief we mean evidence for a belief, then we may be able to make sense of the idea of believing without a reason. If this is not only psychologically possible but rationally desirable, then, odd as it may sound, it may be '*reasonable*' to hold a belief for which one has no reasons.

Once again, to make sense of this possibility, we must put some restrictions on how the term 'evidence' is defined. If, for example, we define 'evidence' so broadly that the simple fact that a belief seems true to a person is counted as evidence for the truth of the belief, then there may be no beliefs people hold for which they do not have some evidence. Or, if we say that whatever it is that makes the truth of a proposition evident to a person counts as evidence, even if what fulfils that role is something, such as a physiological process, of which the person is unaware, then there may be no such thing as belief without evidence. If, however, by 'evidence' we mean to refer to some fact or facts of which a person is aware and from which the belief in question is derived through some process of conscious inference, then there do seem to be beliefs without evidence.

In fact, such beliefs seem not only possible but inescapable, given one familiar line of philosophical argument. Surely it is true that some of my beliefs are held on the basis of other beliefs that function as evidence. Thus, I believe that one of my students is highly intelligent. I hold this belief because I believe that this student is the author of certain philosophical papers that could only have been written by a highly intelligent person. But why do I hold the beliefs that this student is the author of those papers and that the papers are the kind that display high intelligence? I may have evidence for these beliefs as well. For example, I may hold that the fact that the student handed in the papers to me and placed her name upon them is good inductive evidence that she wrote them, because the great majority of papers received in this way are written by the people whose names are on them. And of course I may have evidence for those new beliefs in turn.

Eventually, however, if the chain of evidential reasons is not going to be infinitely long, it seems that I must believe some things without believing those things on the basis of any other beliefs. It may be that in some broad sense of 'evidence' I have evidence for these foundational or basic beliefs, but such evidence could not consist of other propositional beliefs from which the basic beliefs are inferred, or else the basic beliefs would not be basic. So it seems plausible that not all our beliefs can be based on other beliefs, and thus that not all our beliefs can be based on propositional evidence. Presumably, then, some of our beliefs are not only basic, but properly so, in the sense that the person holding the belief not based on any other beliefs has not violated any epistemic duty and is not guilty of any intellectual failing.

Of course it does not follow from this that any religious beliefs will fall into the category of being properly basic beliefs. However, it does mean that the person I will call an *evidentialist*, that is, someone who wants to require that beliefs be based on evidence, will have to state this evidentialist obligation carefully and restrict it in some way. Evidentialism cannot sensibly require that all of our beliefs be based on other beliefs that function as evidence.

For example, the 'ethics of belief' defended by W. K. Clifford in his famous essay by that same title seems too unrestricted. Clifford famously says that 'it is wrong always, everywhere, and for any one, to believe anything upon insufficient evidence'.[1] However, it is hard to see how it can be right to say that all beliefs require sufficient evidence if some beliefs legitimately require no evidence at all. If no evidence at all can count as sufficient evidence, then Clifford's evidentialist requirement would seem to be pretty toothless. One suggestion for Clifford would be to revise his principle so that it only applies to non-basic beliefs and not to beliefs that are properly basic. That of course, would still leave hanging the question as to which beliefs are properly basic and which would require evidence.

Even if we restrict the principle to non-basic beliefs, there is a difficulty in applying Clifford's principle in an even-handed way to various regions of human belief. Clifford states his evidentialist principle in a way that makes it appear that it applies to all fields of human intellectual inquiry. Nevertheless, it is widely accepted that Clifford has religious beliefs in mind as his chief polemical target, because of a sense that religious believers are the greatest sinners in this area. However, it seems highly dubious that religious beliefs are uniquely deficient when measured by some kind of evidentialist standard. It is true that lots of well-informed, apparently rational people who know all of the relevant facts appear to disagree about religious questions, and this might suggest that many or all of them do not have adequate evidence for their beliefs. However, Peter van Inwagen, in an important essay on Clifford, has argued that this critical attitude towards religious beliefs reflects a double standard.[2] People who think that religious beliefs are uniquely problematic either think that religious beliefs fare worse than other kinds of beliefs when examined with respect to their evidential base, or else think that religious beliefs need to be held to a higher standard than other kinds. When we actually compare religious beliefs with other kinds, these claims appear dubious, however.

The other kinds of beliefs to which van Inwagen compares religious beliefs are political and philosophical beliefs. In these areas, just as in religion, people who are equally intelligent, reasonable and informed hold divergent beliefs about important questions. We have the same reason that we have in the case of religion to think that such people lack sufficient evidence. Yet most do not think that we must accept some kind of general scepticism about political and philosophical beliefs. Some people believe strongly in limiting government power; others believe strongly that governments must become more active in working for the common good. Both kinds of people may be justified in holding their beliefs. It seems wrong then to say that religious beliefs always fare worse than other kinds when measured by the need for evidence, and we surely need some justification for the claim that religious beliefs should be held to a higher standard than these other kinds.

Therefore, I conclude that Clifford's principle is not necessarily damaging to religious beliefs. Perhaps people who hold particular political and philosophical beliefs do have sufficient evidence for them; it is just that for some reason they are unable to communicate the force of that evidence to others. If that is so in the case of political and philosophical beliefs, it might be true in the case of religious beliefs as well. Religious people might also have evidence which they cannot communicate. If, however, people who hold particular political and philosophical beliefs do not have sufficient evidence for them, and yet seem justified in holding such beliefs, then it appears that Clifford's principle, even if restricted to non-basic beliefs, is an unreasonable one, and in that case it is hard to see why it should be applied to religious beliefs either.

If van Inwagen is right, then the religious believer should not find Clifford's claim to be very disturbing. There are two possible lines of response. One is to argue that religious believers do have evidence, the same kinds of evidence that people have in other regions of beliefs where there are ongoing disputes between reasonable people. The other response is to challenge the claim that religious beliefs need to be rooted in evidence. It is this second line of response that I wish to pursue in the remainder of this chapter. Why should we think that religious beliefs must meet some kind of evidentialist requirement?

George Mavrodes has helpfully pointed out that evidentialist requirements come in two different forms.[3] Clifford's requirement seems to be what Mavrodes calls a *threshold* requirement. Though Clifford does not say what counts as sufficient evidence, he seems to think there is a certain amount of evidence beyond which belief is justified. This is quite different from a *proportionality* requirement, which is defended in different forms by both John Locke and David Hume.[4] A proportionality requirement thinks of belief as something that comes in degrees and demands that the degree of belief be proportioned in some way to the strength of the evidence. In principle, this is quite different from a threshold requirement, since such a threshold requirement says nothing about the degree of belief appropriate for those beliefs that meet or exceed the threshold. Also, depending on where the threshold is set, one can easily imagine beliefs not based on strong evidence that fall short of the threshold, and thus should not be believed at all if one goes by the threshold requirement, that nevertheless deserve some form of weak belief on the proportionality requirement.

Since evidentialism comes in these two forms, it follows that its denial can take various forms as well. An anti-evidentialist, for example, could deny the threshold requirement by claiming that some beliefs do not need evidence that exceeds the threshold. One form this dispute might take is a disagreement over what beliefs can be properly basic, with an evidentialist claiming that a particular kind of belief stands in need of evidence, in contrast to the anti-evidentialist who maintains that this type of belief can be properly basic and needs no evidence at all. Another kind of anti-evidentialist might deny the proportionality requirement by claiming that the strength of a belief need not be directly linked to the strength of the evidence. The second kind of anti-evidentialist might reject the first kind of evidentialism as well, but it also seems possible for this second kind of anti-evidentialist to accept some kind of threshold requirement and thus accept the first kind of evidentialism.

A fully-fledged evidentialism obviously requires answers to a number of questions. Both kinds must specify what is to count as evidence, and also specify what kinds of beliefs are non-basic and thus stand in need of evidence. Questions must be answered about the degree of control people have over their beliefs if the evidentialist requirement is to be a normative, ethical one. A threshold evidentialist must explain whether there is a single threshold for all kinds of beliefs, and where the threshold, whether it is unitary or not, falls. A proportionality evidentialist must explain what 'degree of belief' amounts to and what kind of function there is that allows degree of belief to be determined by evidence.

I wish to discuss two philosophers who have challenged evidentialist requirements for religious beliefs. The two philosophers in question are William James, who wrote a classic essay, 'The Will to Believe', in response to W. K. Clifford,[5] and Alvin Plantinga, who has written 'Reason and Belief in God', a much-discussed defence of the claim that religious beliefs can be 'properly basic'.[6] Both James and Plantinga have been accused of being fideists, and so it seems important to see if there is anything in their views that is both defensible and deserves to be called fideism. I shall discuss Plantinga as challenging threshold evidentialism, and look at James as an example of a thinker who challenges proportionality evidentialism. Since I want to consider threshold evidentialism first, I shall look at the two thinkers in reverse chronological order and discuss Plantinga's work first.

PLANTINGA'S ARGUMENT THAT RELIGIOUS BELIEFS CAN BE PROPERLY BASIC

I have argued above that a sensible form of threshold evidentialism must restrict the evidentialist requirement to non-basic beliefs. Thus, any demand that religious beliefs be based on evidence assumes that religious beliefs cannot be properly basic. It is precisely this assumption that Alvin Plantinga criticises in his essay 'Reason and Belief in God'. In this essay Plantinga does not distinguish between threshold and proportionality evidentialism, though since he refers to both Clifford and Hume he may intend to reject both. However, regardless of his polemical intent, we can characterise Plantinga's aim positively. It is to defend what he calls the claim of the Protestant reformers that 'it is entirely right, rational, reasonable, and proper to believe in God without any evidence or argument at all'.[7] It seems to me that this is a direct challenge to the threshold form of evidentialism, at least if this evidentialism is committed to the claim that all religious beliefs must be based on evidence.

In passing, it may be remarked that Plantinga could consistently accept some kind of proportionality evidentialism for non-basic beliefs; such a requirement would not contradict the view that religious beliefs were properly basic. In one place he approvingly cites Reformed thinkers who show no objections to the claim that non-basic beliefs should be proportioned to 'support from the foundations'.[8] However, the real dispute again concerns whether or not particular beliefs can be properly basic, since it is possible that Plantinga might accept a threshold requirement for non-basic beliefs as well. In any case I shall discuss Plantinga's essay as an attack on the threshold requirement as this is applied to belief in God.

Plantinga clearly believes that some form of *foundationalism* in epistemology is correct. That is, he accepts the kind of claim I made in the previous section that not all of our beliefs can be based on other beliefs, but rather some of them are properly basic. What he terms the evidentialist objection to religious belief is the claim that religious beliefs are among those for which evidence is required, and yet for which adequate evidence is lacking.[9] Plantinga is careful not to say that one cannot provide evidence for belief in God. However, he wants to deny that such evidence is necessary for belief in God to be proper. So, in his terminology, he is attacking the evidentialist claim that religious beliefs need to be based on evidence and is instead claiming that such beliefs can be properly basic.

The evidentialist who is Plantinga's opponent does not then deny that there are such things as properly basic beliefs, but rather denies that belief in God is one of those properly basic beliefs. But why should belief in God not be basic? According to Plantinga, the evidentialists have typically rested their case on what he terms *classical foundationalism* in epistemology. Obviously, one cannot allow just any belief to be properly basic. How do we decide which ones are entitled to basicality? The classical foundationalist, on Plantinga's reading, says that properly basic beliefs must be either 'self-evident or incorrigible or evident to the senses'.[10] Since belief in God does not appear to meet any of these requirements, the classical foundationalist naturally thinks that it must be one of those beliefs for which evidence is required.

As Plantinga sees it, this criterion of proper basicality is open to obvious counter-objections. Many propositions are properly basic which do not meet these requirements. He cites, for example, the proposition, 'I had lunch this noon'. Plantinga argues that this proposition is not believed on the basis of any others and that he is entirely rational to believe it in this basic way, even though it is neither self-evident, incorrigible, or evident to the senses.[11]

Even more devastating, the classical foundationalist view is self-referentially incoherent. Classical foundationalism is committed to something like the following principle: a proposition is rationally acceptable to a person only if it either meets the classical foundationalist criterion for proper basicality, or else can be derived from properly basic propositions that do meet the criterion by means that measure up to the same standards (being self-evident, incorrigible or evident to the senses).[12] However, this principle does not itself measure up to this standard. The claim that a proposition is rationally acceptable only if it is either self-evident, incorrigible, or evident to the senses or else can be derived in a certain manner from propositions that are in this category is not itself self-evident, incorrigible, or evident to the senses. Nor does it seem at all plausible that an argument for this principle can be derived from propositions that are self-evident, incorrigible, or evident to the senses. Hence it is irrational for anyone to accept the classical foundationalist view of what is rationally acceptable, since if one accepted the theory one would also have an obligation to reject it.

So Plantinga rejects the classical foundationalist account of proper basicality and rational acceptability. Still, he would agree with the classical foundationalist that one should not allow just any proposition to be properly basic. However, Plantinga does not offer any general criteria for proper basicality. In fact, he argues specifically that such criteria do not have to be accepted before a person can make any judgments about what is properly basic. Rather, he argues that we must proceed in a broadly inductive manner here if we are to develop any criteria, and 'assemble examples of beliefs and conditions such that the former are obviously properly basic in the latter, and examples of beliefs and conditions such that the former are obviously *not* properly basic in the latter'.[13]

Furthermore, there is no reason to think that everyone will agree on the relevant set of examples. Some Christians will suppose that belief in God as properly basic is entirely rational. 'Followers of Bertrand Russell and Madelyn Murray O'Hare may disagree; but how is that relevant'?[14] Plantinga argues that the Christian community is entitled to use its own set of examples.

It is this claim that Plantinga uses to defuse what he refers to as the 'great pumpkin' objection. In response to the claim that belief in God can be properly basic, some object that this opens the door to allowing just any belief to be properly basic and therefore rational. It would seem, for example, that a believer in the great pumpkin could argue that this belief is properly basic and therefore stands in no need of evidence. Plantinga responds that just because religious believers cannot provide general criteria for proper basicality it does not follow that they hold that just any belief is properly basic. Rather, the believer will hold that there is a relevant difference between the great pumpkin and God. Belief in God is properly basic on Plantinga's view, because it has a *ground*. (I will say more about grounds below.) We believe in God in certain circumstances because God has implanted within humans a natural tendency or mechanism to believe in him in those circumstances. There is no ground for belief in the great pumpkin since there is no great pumpkin and no natural tendency implanted in us by the great pumpkin to believe in him.[14]

GROUNDS FOR BELIEF AND EXTERNALISM

The notion of a *ground* in the above account is quite important. It is obvious for Plantinga that a ground for a belief is not necessarily evidence for a belief, since he holds that belief in God which is not based on evidence still has a ground. However, a ground, like evidence, seems to be something that confers justification on a belief.[16] How then are the two different?

It seems to me that Plantinga thinks of evidence as something that is propositional in character, which provides a basis for another proposition by some form of inference or argument. Normally, at least, evidence for me is another belief of which I am aware or of which I can easily become aware. Furthermore, it is important that I am also aware of the way the evidential belief supports the belief for which it functions as evidence. These two conditions suggest that a belief based on evidence is one that at least partially conforms to the requirements of epistemological *internalism*.

The internalist thinks that what a person knows must be determined by 'internal' factors, that is, factors of which the individual is conscious or can easily become conscious. For example, internalists typically claim that to know a proposition, I must be aware of the evidence for that proposition, be aware that the evidence is evidence for the proposition, and be aware that it is good evidence.

A ground in Plantinga's sense does not appear to measure up to all of these internalist requirements. Plantinga gives the following as examples of grounds: A person contemplates a flower and then immediately forms the belief 'This flower was created by God'. A person contemplates the starry heavens and immediately forms the belief 'This vast and intricate universe was created by God'.[17] It is true that the individual in question has some kind of conscious experience or awareness that is part of the ground, and it might seem that this favours internalism. But it is important to see that the ground of the belief in these cases is not simply the experience, but rather the total circumstances of the believer. The ground is not properly thought of as a belief at all, or even as an experience, but rather as a set of circumstances which includes an experience of a certain kind. Moreover, there is no conscious inference or argument in these cases. The individual is simply constituted in such a way that when certain experiences occur in certain circumstances, particular beliefs are immediately formed. The circumstances in these cases function as grounds by virtue of the fact that God is said to have created the mechanisms by which these beliefs are formed.

There is an analogy here to ordinary perceptual beliefs. In the normal case, when I see a book in front of me, I form the belief that there is a book spontaneously or immediately. I do *not* reason as follows: 'I am having the experience one typically has when there is a book in front of one; therefore there probably is a book in front of me'. Rather, when I am in the appropriate circumstances, I simply find myself forming the belief that there is a book in front of me.

One can see then that Plantinga is implicitly committed to an *externalist* epistemology, a commitment that becomes explicit in his later series of books on warrant.[18] Externalism holds that whether a belief constitutes knowledge is not completely a function of the truth of the belief plus things of which the individual is consciously aware, but is at least partly determined by how the individual is in fact related to the external world, regardless of whether or not the individual is aware of that relation. Plantinga's account of grounds is externalist because whether belief in God is grounded depends on whether or not God exists and has implanted in humans a natural mechanism to believe in him in certain circumstances. If this condition holds, then in those circumstances belief in God is grounded, regardless of whether or not the individual knows or believes anything about the relevant mechanism. In his books on warrant, Plantinga goes on to argue explicitly that beliefs that do not meet internalist requirements can be knowledge. Specifically, he claims that a true belief will be knowledge when it is the outcome of a human cognitive faculty designed to obtain truth, when that faculty is operating reliably in accordance with its design plan in the circumstances in which it is designed to operate.[19] One can easily see that on this theory, a belief in God that is the outcome of a God-implanted mechanism designed to produce belief in God could not only be properly basic, but could be knowledge.

IS PLANTINGA'S VIEW FIDEISTIC?

Plantinga's view is often characterised as a form of fideism. Not surprisingly, since fideism is commonly used as a term of abuse, he denies that this is so. He argues in the final section of 'Reason and Belief in God' that his position is not best thought of as a form of fideism, though he admits that whether the label is appropriate will depend on how the term is defined. Plantinga appeals to a dictionary definition of fideism as 'exclusive or basic reliance upon faith alone, accompanied by a consequent disparagement of reason'[20] and argues with some justice that his view does not commit him to anything like fideism in this sense. In fact, Plantinga argues that on his account, the proposition 'God exists' turns out to be something that one can know by reason, since he regards what can be known through our natural cognitive faculties as what can be known by reason, and he is arguing that belief in God's existence results from just such a faculty.[21]

However, as Plantinga himself notes, there are various ways in which fideism might be defined. He acknowledges that his claim that belief in God is knowable by reason is one that many non-theistic philosophers will reject. The disagreement between himself and such philosophers is not, he says, that they both agree about what can be known by reason, but then disagree about what should be believed. Rather, he says, they disagree about what can be known by reason; perhaps they even have 'different conceptions of reason'.[22]

This may not be fideism in the dictionary sense cited, but it does appear to be fideistic in some other senses. First of all, and most obviously, Plantinga is arguing that religious beliefs can be legitimately held without any reasons in the sense of evidence. If fideism is defined as a claim that religious beliefs may legitimately be held without evidence, then this is clearly fideistic. Secondly, Plantinga's claims are closely related to one of the themes that I discussed in the first two chapters as a source of fideism:

the 'no neutrality' thesis. If fideism is defined as a denial that human reason can be completely objective or neutral with respect to questions like the existence of God, then Plantinga's view seems once more fideistic. Insofar as fideism is simply a term of abuse, it is natural for Plantinga to disavow the term, but such a disavowal is consistent with a recognition that in some other senses his views may indeed be fideistic, along with an insistence that in those senses, fideism is defensible.

The elements in Plantinga's thought that strike some critics as fideistic are related, I think, to its externalism. Externalism is really a repudiation of a certain kind of epistemological project that has been dominant in modern philosophy. This is the project of wishing to give an account of knowledge that would be independent of any particular knowledge claims, so as to provide a foundation for knowledge claims. The externalist denies that this is possible. According to the externalist, to know what knowledge is and how knowledge is possible, we must begin by assuming that we know some things. (Some internalists admit this as well.) What we actually know depends on our actual relations to the world, and if we do not think we know some things about that relation we could never know that we know anything.

This is particularly evident for 'second-level knowledge', that is, knowing that I know something. So, for the externalist, I now know that I am sitting in my office. But do I know that I know that? Whether I know that I am sitting in my office, as opposed to being a brain in a vat being fed electrical impulses that simulate the experiences I would have if I were in my office, depends on whether I am hooked up to the world in the right kind of way. Internally, there may be no difference between my actual situation and the experiences I would have if I were a brain in a vat. If I think that I do know I am in my office, it is because I think that I am hooked up to the world in the right kind of way. There is a kind of circularity present when I ask myself how I know what I know.[23] I cannot certify that this knowledge is genuine knowledge without assuming some knowledge of the same general sort. I could not, for example, test my sensory faculties to see if they are reliable without employing those very sense faculties and thus implicitly assuming they are reliable. There is no internal guarantee that I am not mistaken, and my belief that I have knowledge reveals my already-present commitments.

In a similar way, Plantinga's account is an account that depends on commitments the individual already has. In response to the criticism that belief in God needs evidence, Plantinga responds that it may be properly basic. In response to the claim that this implies the great pumpkin could be properly basic, Plantinga argues that this is not so, because there is no great pumpkin to implant a tendency to believe in him, but there is a God who has done this. However, these claims are made from the standpoint of a believer. They show that a person who has a certain set of commitments and therefore sees the world in a certain way may be perfectly reasonable, and, if those commitments give a proper account of how humans are related to reality, that the commitments make possible knowledge. But one could argue that the whole framework is in a certain sense internal to the life of faith, and that this could reasonably be described as a kind of fideism. But if this is fideistic, then so is the atheistic philosopher who adopts a 'naturalistic epistemology' to explain knowledge, while basing that epistemology on a scientific naturalism which is presupposed as known.[24] What appears as fideism is really a consequence of externalism, and there can then be secular counterparts to religious fideism.

To say this is not to criticise either Plantinga or the naturalistic epistemologist. If an externalist epistemology is correct, then there may be no alternative to this type of fideism. There may indeed be no completely neutral faculty of human reason, only a reason that functions in the context of certain taken-for-granted commitments.

WILLIAM JAMES AND THE WILL TO BELIEVE

In this chapter I am exploring the idea of fideism as holding certain religious beliefs without evidence. Plantinga provides a clear example of a rejection of 'threshold evidentialism' for religious beliefs. On his view, we do not need any particular amount of evidence to believe in God; we do not need any evidence at all. However, I noted at the beginning of the chapter that there is proportionality evidentialism as well as threshold evidentialism. I now wish to turn to a classic essay by William James, which I shall interpret as an attack on this other kind of evidentialism.

William James wrote his famous essay, 'The Will to Believe', as a rebuttal to W. K. Clifford's essay arguing for an evidentialist point of view. James does not distinguish between threshold evidentialism and proportionality evidentialism, and he almost certainly saw himself as disagreeing with Clifford's position. However, George Mavrodes, in the review of the debate that we have already briefly discussed, shows that if we construe Clifford as a threshold evidentialist, the actual position James puts forward may be consistent with Clifford's view.

As we have already noted, Clifford argues that it is 'wrong always, everywhere, and for every one, to believe anything upon insufficient evidence'. James's response to this is to argue that in certain highly qualified situations, where we face what he calls genuine options, 'our passional nature not only lawfully may, but must decide between propositions'.[25] A genuine option is explained as a case where we are faced with two propositions, and the choice between the two meets three conditions: it must be *live*, *forced* and *momentous*.[26]

A live option is defined as one in which both of two rival hypotheses have enough appeal to the intellect to make belief a real possibility. James thus recognises that many beliefs, perhaps most, are not under our intellectual control. Some of the factors that make an hypothesis live or dead for us are non-rational; they are a function of what views are taken seriously in our culture or sub-culture or family, for example. But strong evidence may also make a particular hypothesis seem certain (or certainly false) for us.

An option is forced when it is based on a logical disjunction, and some choice is unavoidable. James gives as an example of a non-forced option the following: 'Choose between going out with your umbrella or without it'.[26] One can avoid this choice by not going out at all. In the field of religion, 'Either accept Christianity or Hinduism' would similarly fail to be a forced option; there are other alternatives, including agnosticism and other religions. However, 'Either believe there is a God or do not believe there is a God' is a forced option. Here we have an option in the form of 'either accept this truth or go without it' and James says such options are forced.[27]

An option is momentous when some unique opportunity rests on the choice. A chance to go on a polar expedition may be a once in a lifetime opportunity, and the decision to go or not may hinge on a person's beliefs about the character and the skill of the leader. This third condition reveals that for James a belief is not merely an intellectual act of assent; it may include that, but it is also a rule for action.

James argues against Clifford that when all of these three conditions are met, and thus an option is a genuine one, then one cannot avoid belief, since the option is forced. Nor should one want to, since the option is momentous. Moreover, since the option is live, it also follows that there is not enough theoretical evidence to give the intellect a conclusive resolution. In such a situation, James says that what he calls a 'passional preference' is both inescapable and legitimate.

We can now see why Mavrodes is able to argue that James's view does not actually contradict what Clifford says, even though the two philosophers doubtless would think of themselves as disagreeing. Clifford says that we must have 'sufficient evidence' for all of our beliefs. However, he does not say how much evidence is sufficient. Beyond that threshold of sufficiency, belief is justified. Now James does not say that there is no evidence for religious (or anti-religious) beliefs. Rather, he seems to assume that in the case where a religious belief is a genuine option, the evidence pro and con is fairly closely balanced. If the evidence were decisively in one direction or the other, then the option would not be genuine because both hypotheses would not be live. Perhaps, Mavrodes suggests, James's argument is that in the case of a genuine option, balanced evidence of this sort is in fact sufficient for belief.[29] Or, more radically, perhaps belief may be rational even when the evidence is somewhat against one option, and thus somewhat unbalanced evidence may be sufficient.[30]

The relevance of our 'passional nature' in such a case is linked to what Mavrodes calls the 'meatloaf factor'.[31] Suppose you have some left-over meatloaf in your house. It has been in your refrigerator for several days, and unexpected guests appear. Suppose that on the evidence available, the likelihood of the meatloaf being spoiled is about 50 per cent. In that situation you should not form the belief that it is okay and serve it; in fact, even if the evidence is somewhat in favour of the meatloaf being okay, a reasonable person will decide not to trust it.

In this case there is a 'value asymmetry' that favours scepticism about the meatloaf. However, Mavrodes suggests that in other cases there might be a 'value asymmetry' that cuts in favour of belief and against scepticism, and that James is arguing that this is sometimes true in cases of religious belief.[32]

Interpreted in this way, James's argument actually bears some similarity to the famous 'wager' argument from the seventeenth-century French mathematician and philosopher, Blaise Pascal.[33] Pascal developed his argument on the assumption that reason could neither prove nor disprove the existence of God, and yet that some kind of decision about belief is required, because the belief is one that is crucial for life. 'Yes, but you must wager. It is not optional. You are embarked.'[34] If one thinks about the decision from the point of view of a gambler, Pascal says the choice is an easy one:

> Let us weigh the gain and the loss in wagering that God is. Let us estimate these two chances. If you gain, you gain all; if you lose, you lose nothing. Wager, then, without hesitation that He is.[35]

Pascal, like James, thinks of the decision as a forced option, and one in which the 'meatloaf factor' (an asymmetry in the value of the consequences of belief and doubt) is strongly at work.[36] He reasons that if God exists and one establishes a relation with God, the reward is infinite: eternal life. If one bets that God does not exist, and there really is a God, one stands then to lose an infinite good. But what if one is wrong and there is no God? In that case, one can at most lose a few years of sinful pleasures. In reality,

Pascal thinks there is little or no payoff even if there is no God and one correctly bets on atheism, since he assumes that the person of faith will be 'faithful, honest, humble, grateful, generous, a sincere friend, truthful' and that a life characterised by such qualities will be superior to the 'poisonous pleasure' of unbelief in any case.[37]

Pascal has an interesting reply to the person who admits that belief would be desirable but finds himself or herself unable to believe:

> Endeavour then to convince yourself, not by increase of proofs of God, but by the abatement of your passions. You would like to attain faith, and do not know the way; you would like to cure yourself of unbelief, and ask the remedy for it. Learn of those who have been bound like you, and who now stake all their possessions. These are people who know the way which you would follow, and who are cured of an ill of which you would be cured. Follow the ways by which they began; by acting as if they believed . . .[38]

Pascal's emphasis here on the passions anticipates some of the themes of Søren Kierkegaard that will be discussed in Chapter 7.

To return to James himself, he argues that the goals of our intellectual life could be summed up in the duties to believe truth and to avoid error.[39] However, James points out that these two goals are not equivalent. We could maximise truths believed by believing as many propositions as possible; we could minimise error by believing as little as possible. Which we decide to do will depend on whether we value more highly the gaining of truth or the avoiding of error.[40] James says that since we are certain to make some errors, he is personally willing to run some risks for the sake of truth.[41] However, he could have added that what counts is not merely whether we value gaining truth more than avoiding error, but the importance of the truths we are seeking. Mavrodes points out that I could easily acquire many truths to believe; I could, for example, count the words on a page in the newspaper and I would have a new item of knowledge if I count carefully. But no one thinks it worthwhile to accumulate truths in this way. Rather, it seems that it is the importance of the truths we are seeking that really counts, and this points us back in the direction of something like the 'meatloaf factor'. Such valuational factors may then determine whether the evidence we have in the case of a genuine option is sufficient, even when that evidence is not very powerful.

JAMES AND PROPORTIONALITY EVIDENTIALISM

We have looked at Mavrodes' argument that James's position is actually consistent with threshold evidentialism, at least of a sort. One way of construing the argument is that it shows that in certain cases evidence that is only even, or even somewhat less than even, might be sufficient for belief. However, regardless of what James may think about threshold evidentialism, I believe that his view is a blow against proportionality evidentialism.

If we do think James is arguing that in cases of genuine options, evidence that is less than impressive may be sufficient, it is clear that he does not think that belief in these situations must be strictly proportional to the evidence. In the case where the evidence is balanced, the proportionality rule would appear to require an equal degree of belief on both sides, but that is equivalent to agnosticism, with no definite belief either way. James clearly thinks that there are factors other than evidence that properly bear on strength of belief.

As has often been noted, the notion of strength or degree of belief is not entirely clear. We could mean by 'degree of belief' the degree of certainty or confidence one has about a belief. Alternatively, one could understand degree of belief as the degree of willingness one might have to abandon a belief in the face of new evidence. These two factors are not the same. I might feel very certain about a belief, say my belief about what I had for breakfast this morning, yet abandon that belief very quickly in the face of new evidence that my memory in this case is faulty. And we can imagine a scientist who has much uncertainty about a particular theory, but who is very reluctant to abandon the theory because of the lack of an alternative, or perhaps because of the great theoretical importance of the belief.

However we understand the idea of 'degree of belief' it is clear that James does not think that evidence is the only factor that ought to shape our degree of belief (even if it clearly is one factor). He gives several examples of cases where it seems unreasonable to allow degree of belief to be determined solely by evidence. One of the clearest is found in a companion essay to 'The Will to Believe' called 'The Sentiment of Rationality'.[42] Suppose, says James, I am climbing in the Alps and find myself in a dangerous situation from which I can only escape by a terrible leap. The evidence that I can make the leap may not be too great, though by the argument already made, it may be sufficient to justify belief. However, James points out that I am much more likely to be successful if I hold the belief with great confidence. In this case, I should not only believe, but believe with all the confidence I can muster.[43]

One might think that this case would not be analogous to cases of religious belief, but James argues that social relationships are among the areas where beliefs cannot be strictly determined by evidence. If I hope to develop a friendship, I must often find myself trusting and believing the friend with a firmness that the evidence I already have would not warrant.[44] If we think that the religious life is also social in nature, involving the development of a friendship with God, then similar conclusions may hold.[45]

One might object to James's claims on the basis that what he really shows is that actions can rationally be performed that are the actions one might perform if one were to hold a certain belief. Thus, what James justifies is not belief but acting as if one held a belief. However, James himself would not admit that such a dichotomy between belief and action exists. It is true that people can fail to act on their beliefs, but it is also true that sometimes people do not really believe what they think they believe. And one way our true beliefs can come out is by what actions we perform when we are put to the test. Furthermore, psychologists have shown that in the long run, people tend to shift their beliefs to make them consistent with their actions. Hence, someone who advises me to act as if I believed a certain proposition is in effect advising me to act in such a way that I will, in all probability, come to form the belief in question.

CONCLUSION: FAITH WITHOUT REASONS

We have looked at Plantinga's argument that belief in God may be properly basic and thus not based on reasons at all, as well as James's argument that religious beliefs may be based on evidence that is less than conclusive, and yet be held with a strength that is not solely a function of the somewhat meagre evidence. Both argue that in some cases this belief that is not strictly governed by reasons in the sense of evidence is reasonable. But if they are right in arguing for the reasonableness of such a belief policy, are they really fideists? If fideism is the rejection of reason, the answer is clearly no. However, I have already argued that fideism as the rejection of reason is an indefensible position. It seems to me that what Plantinga and James are defending is an important part of what is sometimes called fideism, and thus they may legitimately be called fideists of a kind. Perhaps we should call fideism that can be rationally defended *responsible fideism*. In the succeeding chapters, I shall look at some more varieties of responsible fideism by analysing other fideistic claims: specifically, the claims that faith may be *above* reason and even that it may in some sense be *against* reason.

NOTES

1. W. K. Clifford, 'The Ethics of Belief', in *The Ethics of Belief Debate*, ed. Gerald D. McCarthy (Atlanta, Georgia: Scholars Press, 1986) p. 24.
2. Peter van Inwagen. 'It is Wrong, Everywhere, Always, and for Anyone, to Believe Anything upon Insufficient Evidence', in Jeff Jordan and Daniel Howard-Snyder (eds), *Faith, Freedom and Rationality* (Lanham, Maryland: Rowman and Littlefield, 1996).

3. George Mavrodes, 'Intellectual Morality in Clifford and James', in *The Ethics of Belief Debate*, pp. 207–9.
4. See John Locke, *An Essay Concerning Human Understanding*, ed. Peter H. Nidditch (Oxford: Oxford University Press, 1975) 4. 15. 5 (p. 656). Also see David Hume's claim that 'a wise man proportions his belief to the evidence', in *An Enquiry Concerning Human Understanding*, ed. Eric Steinberg (Indianapolis, Indiana: Hackett Publishing Co., 1993) Section X, p. 73.
5. William James's essay has been frequently anthologised but first appeared in *The Will to Believe and Other Essays in Popular Philosophy* (New York: Longmans, Green and Co., 1897) pp. 1–31.
6. Alvin Plantinga, 'Reason and Belief in God', in *Faith and Rationality*, ed. Alvin Plantinga and Nicholas Wolterstorff (Notre Dame, Indiana: University of Notre Dame Press, 1983).
7. Plantinga, p. 17.
8. Plantinga, p. 72.
9. Plantinga, p. 29.
10. Plantinga, p. 60.
11. Ibid.
12. Plantinga, p. 61. I have simplified the wording of Plantinga's own statement of this argument for clarity of exposition.
13. Plantinga, p. 76.
14. Plantinga, p. 77.
15. Plantinga, p. 74.
16. In his later works, Plantinga makes a distinction between justification and warrant, that quality that converts a true belief into knowledge, but this distinction is not present in 'Reason and Belief in God'. See Plantinga, p. 91.
17. Plantinga, p. 80.
18. See Alvin Plantinga, *Warrant: The Current Debate* (New York: Oxford University Press, 1993) and *Warrant and Proper Function* (New York: Oxford University Press, 1993).
19. See Plantinga, *Warrant and Proper Function*, pp. 46–7 for a more precise statement of his account.
20. Plantinga, 'Reason and Belief in God', p. 87.
21. Plantinga, pp. 89–90.
22. Plantinga, p. 90.
23. For a good account of the circularity inherent in externalist accounts of second-level knowledge, see William Alston, 'On Knowing that We Know: The Application to Religious Knowledge', in *Christian Perspectives on Religious Knowledge*, ed. C. Stephen Evans and Merold Westphal (Grand Rapids, Michigan: Wm B. Eerdmans, 1993) pp. 15–39.
24. For a classic example, see W. V. O. Quine's essay, 'Epistemology Naturalized', in *Ontological Relativity and Other Essays* (New York: Columbia University Press, 1969).
25. William James, 'The Will to Believe', p. 11.
26. James, pp. 2–4.
27. James, p. 3.
28. Ibid.
29. Mavrodes, p. 214.
30. Mavrodes, p. 215.
31. Mavrodes, p. 213.
32. Ibid.
33. Pascal's argument can be found in his *Penseés*, section 233. See *Pascal's Penseés*, trans. W. F. Trotter (New York: E. P. Dutton and Co., 1958) pp. 65–9.
34. Pascal, p. 66.
35. Pascal, p. 67.
36. For more on Pascal's wager argument, see Chapter 9 of Stephen T. Davis, *God, Reason and Theistic Proofs* (Edinburgh: Edinburgh University Press, 1997) in the same series as the present book. Davis also includes a very interesting treatment of William James's argument as well. A number of illuminating essays on Pascal's wager can be found in Jeff Jordan (ed.), *Gambling on God: Essays on Pascal's Wager* (Lanham, Maryland: Rowman and Littlefield, 1994).
37. Pascal, p. 68.
38. Pascal, p. 68.
39. James, p. 18.
40. James, pp. 18–19.
41. James, pp. 26–7.

42. William James, 'The Sentiment of Rationality', in *The Will to Believe and Other Essays*, pp. 63–110.
43. James, 'The Sentiment of Rationality', pp. 96–7.
44. James, 'The Will to Believe', pp. 23–4.
45. James, 'The Will to Believe', pp. 27–8.

4

Faith Above Reason: Aquinas

Responsible fideism may seem to be a paradoxical notion. If fideism involves the denigration of reason, then how can there be a rational fideism? The answer lies in the possibility of reason becoming self-critical. If human reason has limitations and also has some ability to recognise those limitations, then the possibility of responsible fideism emerges.

In Chapter 2 I argued that fideism as the claim that faith is completely autonomous or immune from rational scrutiny is not an attractive position. In the last chapter I sketched a kind of responsible fideism by looking at the possibility of belief *without* reasons. However, this discussion did not inquire as to why faith without reasons might be good or even necessary. One possible answer to this question involves the content of what is believed. Perhaps faith requires belief without reasons because the content of the belief is such that human reason cannot fully understand it. One way such a claim has often been made is to assert that faith requires beliefs that are in some sense *above* reason.

In fact, the claim that faith is above reason is so pervasive in the Christian tradition that one might argue that it is implausible to regard it as a fideistic claim. Since fideism is often used as a term of abuse, few theologians have welcomed this label. Yet most Christian theologians and philosophers have maintained that Christian faith requires some beliefs that are above reason. Such a claim is so mainstream that there appears to be nothing fideistic about it. For example, as we shall see, Thomas Aquinas, often regarded as a rationalist about faith and reason and almost never as a fideist, clearly affirms that faith requires some beliefs that are above reason.

However, the claim that there are truths that humans should believe that are above reason is not completely untroubling. Many contemporary thinkers find such a claim irrational if not unintelligible. Furthermore, some thinkers who are usually cited as fideists, such as Kierkegaard, clearly view the claim that faith is above reason as central to their understanding of the relation of faith to reason. So, despite the fact that many people who are not regarded as fideists make a claim that faith is above reason, we must still investigate this claim in order to understand what might be meant by 'fideism'. Moreover, it is a claim that deserves investigation in its own right, for it is far from obvious what is meant by the assertion that faith is above reason or how such a view might be defended.

One way to categorise different accounts of how faith might be said to be above reason would be to look at the particular propositions that are claimed to be above reason. For example, one theologian might hold that the existence of God is something above reason that must be accepted by faith. Another might regard God's reality as knowable by reason, but claim that God's character as three-in-one is above reason. I will give some examples below of the ways in which Thomas Aquinas distinguishes in this way between truths knowable only by faith and truths that may be known by reason.

However, apart from this kind of difference of opinion about what particular propositions are said to be above reason, there are also differences in what might be meant by making such claims at all. Here are some of the alternatives: 1. The claim that some belief is above reason might mean that although reason can investigate the truth or falsity of a belief, it is not capable of definitively determining its truth or falsity. 2. Somewhat more radically, the claim that a belief is above reason might be taken to mean that though reason can grasp the sense of a belief, reason is not capable of investigating the belief at all. 3. Most radically of all, the claim that a belief is above reason might be taken to mean that reason is not capable of understanding the belief because reason cannot grasp its sense. For example, this might be because reason cannot grasp some important concept that is essential to the belief in question.

These three interpretations are nested in the sense that (3) might be thought to entail (2), and (2) to entail (1). If reason is not capable of understanding a belief, then it seems plausible that reason cannot investigate it either, and of course, if reason cannot investigate the truth of a belief at all, it seems incapable of determining the truth of the belief by such an investigation. However, there is an asymmetry in that it seems possible for (1) to hold without (2), and (2) without (3). One might be able to investigate a belief without being able to determine its truth, and one might still be able to understand a belief in some sense of 'understand' even if one cannot investigate its truth. In the rest of this chapter, I shall look at the medieval philosopher, Thomas Aquinas, as an example of the first possibility. The next two chapters will examine Immanuel Kant and Søren Kierkegaard as illustrations of the second and third options respectively.

This discussion of Aquinas should not be taken as implying that I am claiming that Aquinas should be classified as a fideist. In reality, the question of whether this label does or does not apply to a particular thinker is not a very interesting one, in view of the different things that are meant by the term 'fideism'. Given the pejorative and irrationalist connotations 'fideism' has to many people, calling Aquinas a fideist would be jarring indeed. However, this should not prevent us from looking at themes or elements in the thought of Aquinas that seem fideistic in some sense, and that is what I propose to do in this chapter. If we wish to rehabilitate fideism, or develop a responsible version of it, we may have to look to writers who are not ordinarily looked upon as fideistic.

FAITH IN PROPOSITIONS WHOSE TRUTH CANNOT BE DETERMINED BY REASON: THOMAS AQUINAS ON FAITH IN REVEALED TRUTH

Thomas Aquinas provides us with a classical example of the view that faith involves belief in propositions whose truth cannot be determined by reason alone. Aquinas could perhaps also be cited as illustrating our other two interpretations of the formula of faith as above reason. For instance, he claims that God's essence cannot be known by a human mind by virtue of its natural powers. 'Therefore, a created intellect cannot see the essence of God unless God by His grace unites Himself to the created intellect, as an object made intelligible to it'.[1] Our human inability to know God's essence implies that a human being cannot know God's essence 'unless he be uplifted out of this mortal life'.[2] So for Aquinas in a central way God remains *radically* 'above' human reason; since we cannot grasp God's essence there are truths about God we cannot even understand in our current condition. So for some truths about God, Aquinas would serve as a good illustration of the third or most radical interpretation of the formula 'faith as above reason'. He holds that there are many truths about God that we simply cannot understand at all. Even those truths about God that we can understand are either negative in character, or else are characterised by Aquinas as 'analogical', meaning that we thereby understand something about God insofar as God is related to his creation, rather than understanding God's own essence.[3]

Despite this somewhat radical view of the limits of human reason, Aquinas is well known for his view that there are truths that human beings can grasp about God in this life and that these truths fall into two distinct categories. There are truths about God, such as that God exists and that God is one, which may be revealed but 'which the natural reason also is able to reach'.[4] There are other truths about God 'that exceed all the ability of the human reason', such as that God is triune.[5] We can, for example, know by reason that God created the heavens and the earth in the sense that he is the ultimate cause of their being and of all motion within them, but it is only by faith that we can know that the universe had a beginning in time and that God's creative activity is not an eternal act by which an eternal world is made to be.[6]

Despite our ignorance of God's essence, Aquinas holds that human reason can know some things about God by reasoning from the created order to God as the cause of that created order. There is a real relationship between God and the creation, and that relation allows humans to obtain a kind of 'relational' knowledge of God. Some of these truths that in principle can be known by reason are also revealed by God and can and should be accepted by faith. However, faith also enables us to grasp truths that could not be known by reason at all, such as the fact that God created the world in such a manner that it had a beginning.

Many other examples of truths of both kinds are given by Aquinas. We can by reason know that God is one, that God has no body, that God has no unrealised potential, that he is eternal, and that God's being and essence are identical.[7] However, it is only by faith in revelation that God can be known as a Trinity, in which Father, Son and Holy Spirit can be known as distinct persons.[8]

For Aquinas, these truths that must be grasped by faith are not really *known* by faith, at least if we translate his term '*scientia*' as 'knowledge'. *Scientia* is a kind of theoretical knowledge that requires a truth either to be directly 'seen' as a first principle, or else to be deduced from such certain first principles. Nevertheless, though faith is not *scientia*, it is a 'kind of knowledge'. It is not knowledge in the strict sense because it does not include a direct vision of the truth of what is believed.[9] Nevertheless, human beings can by faith apprehend 'intelligible truths about God' that they could not know if they relied solely on natural human reasoning.[10]

In what sense are these truths apprehended by faith, that are above reason, really *above* reason? That is, are the truths that are to believed by faith propositions whose truth cannot be determined by rational investigation, or is it rather the case that we cannot investigate these propositions at all? A good case can be made for both options. On the one hand, Aquinas speaks about these truths of faith as ones that surpass 'the whole ability of the human reason'.[11] On the other hand, Aquinas says that though these truths cannot be demonstrated by reason, human reason can 'gather certain likenesses' of the truths of faith, and that the arguments whereby this is possible are 'useful'.[12] I think therefore that when Aquinas says that these truths cannot be investigated by reason, he means that we have no way of definitively determining their truth by reason, not that we cannot consider them in the sense of reflecting on reasons for thinking them true or false. It is not that there are no arguments for human reason to consider, but rather that such arguments are always 'weak' and never demonstrative.[13]

WHY DOES FAITH BELIEVE WHAT IS ABOVE REASON?

There are two kinds of question that are naturally raised about this claim that there are truths above reason that are to be accepted by faith. One is why human beings should accept such truths. The other is why God should reveal such truths and want human beings to accept them.

The answer to the first question is straightforward for Aquinas. When someone who is a trustworthy authority reveals some truth to you, then it is reasonable to accept that authority. God is the most trustworthy authority imaginable, so it is supremely reasonable to believe what God has said. Thus Aquinas sees faith, in its 'inward act',[14] not merely as believing certain truths about God but reasonably believing those truths because God has revealed them. However, Aquinas holds that even though faith is reasonable, since faith is not knowledge, the intellect of the person is not compelled to believe, as it is in a case of strict knowledge. Faith is voluntary in the sense that a person can have reasonable grounds for belief and still refuse to believe.

Who would refuse to believe in such a case? For Aquinas the person who does not will to believe is a person who does not want to know God, who does not will God as his final end. Thus, the motive for the voluntary act of faith is 'believing for the sake of God' or believing so that one can gain that vision of God that is the final end for humans.[15]

This answer to the question of why the individual should believe is still incomplete. It may seem acceptable to say that one should believe what God reveals because God has revealed it, but how can one know what God has revealed? There are numerous alleged revelations from God, so the individual needs to be able to decide which of these candidates are genuinely from God.

Aquinas gives several criteria that are to be used in discerning a genuine revelation. First of all, he says that the divine wisdom 'reveals its own presence, as well as the truth of its teaching and inspiration, by fitting arguments'.[16] At least some of these arguments must take the form of confirming by natural reason the truth of what is revealed. However, not all of the truths in the revelation can be independently confirmed, for Aquinas immediately goes on to say that 'in order to confirm those truths that exceed natural knowledge, it [the divine Wisdom] gives visible manifestation to works that surpass the ability of all nature'.[17]

So revelation for Aquinas, since it includes the two kinds of truths (those knowable by reason and those not knowable) requires at least two different ways by which the genuineness of the revelation can be recognised. There are some truths in revelation that do not exceed natural knowledge, and presumably the independent recognition of those truths would add credibility to the revelation. However, if the truths contained in a revelation all had to be confirmed by natural reason independently, this would make the revelation unnecessary, except perhaps as an educational tool or a device to speed up the recognition of the truth. It would become unnecessary to believe truths in the revelation because they were revealed by God, since they could in principle be believed because known by reason to be true.

Therefore it is proper that Aquinas lays great stress on the second criterion, the requirement that there be accompanying miracles, or 'works that surpass the ability of nature'. Aquinas criticises Islam, for example, on the grounds that its revelation claims are not grounded in supernatural signs. Such a sign 'alone fittingly gives witness to divine inspiration; for a visible action that can be only divine reveals an invisibly inspired teacher of truth'.[18]

Besides these reasons for belief, Aquinas also mentions one other kind of reason, one that I believe receives much greater emphasis in later Protestant thinkers. 'He who believes does have something sufficient inducing him to believe. He is induced by the authority of divine teaching confirmed by miracles, and what is more, by an inward impulse towards God, who invites him. So he does not believe lightly'.[19] Note that this 'inward impulse' is here said to be even more important than the miracles.

It cannot be overemphasised that the function of reason in Aquinas' view is to confirm that a purported revelation really is from God; the ground of belief is not reason, but the willingness to believe what God has said because God has said it. Two people can have the same rational grounds for belief, with one believing and one refusing to believe. Aquinas is sometimes criticised for having a 'propositional' view of faith rather than an account of faith that emphasises a personal relation of trust. However, it is clear that the ground of propositional faith in Aquinas is something like a personal trust of God. The individual believes what God has said because of this trust.

WHY DOES GOD REVEAL WHAT IS ABOVE REASON?

Why should God reveal such truths and expect humans to believe them? For Aquinas the highest good is the knowledge of God, and so a revelation from God about God is a great gift to humans: 'even the most imperfect knowledge about the most noble realities brings the greatest perfection to the soul'.[20] Such a revelation gives humans an understanding that they are 'ordained by the divine Providence towards a higher good than human fragility can experience in the present life'.[21] Such a revelation is the only basis for any real understanding of God in this life. Since human reason in this life cannot grasp God in his essence, it is only by a revelation that transcends human reason that we can grasp God as God truly is: 'Hence, by the fact that some things about God are proposed to man that surpass his reason, there is strengthened in man the view that God is something above what he can think'.[22] Such a revelation also has the valuable function of curbing human presumption, helping humans to see that their reason is indeed finite and limited, and thus preventing them from thinking that their own rational powers should be the final test of truth.[23]

We can see therefore in Aquinas a clear example of how the claim that faith must believe some truths that are above reason focuses our attention on the limits of reason. That reason does have such limits is for Aquinas an obvious fact. We can easily see that some humans, who have more intelligence and education, can understand things that other humans, less fortunate in those respects, cannot. It would be, says Aquinas, folly for a person who is less intelligent and educated to claim that what is known as true by a superior person is false, simply because the less qualified person cannot grasp the truth. Aquinas thinks there are creatures whose rational powers exceed even the wisest humans. When humans recognise their own finitude, they can see that it is the 'acme of stupidity for a man to suspect as false what is divinely revealed through the ministry of the angels simply because it cannot be investigated by reason'.[24]

CAN IT BE RATIONAL FOR REASON TO RECOGNISE ITS LIMITS?

The claim that there are truths above reason that must be accepted by faith clearly implies that human reason has definite limits. It is hard to see how this view of reason as limited can be denied. Even philosophers who are sceptical about the existence of God and angels would concede the possibility, if the not the actuality, of the existence of other intelligent beings somewhere in space whose cognitive abilities vastly exceed those of humans. However, one can still imagine someone objecting in the following way: 'Certainly one must concede the finitude of human reason and the possibility that there are intelligent beings with higher capacities. However, it is not clear how we humans could ever recognise the superiority of such beings, since by hypothesis they can know things that we cannot know. But we can only discern their rational competence by checking out what they claim to know for ourselves. Insofar as we are able to do this successfully, we will be their equal with respect to those particular areas of knowledge. Hence, even if there are beings with higher cognitive powers, we could never show that they are in fact superior, and would never be justified in accepting testimony from them because of this alleged superiority'.

This objection is in fact parallel to an objection that is sometimes made against accepting a divine revelation. The objection begins with the assumption that modern persons are 'autonomous' and must have reasons for belief that can be recognised as valid by the believer. The objection is that a revelation cannot meet this condition and must therefore violate this autonomy. The argument for this is that either we can recognise the truth of the revelation independently or we cannot. If we can do so on our own, then the revelation is unnecessary. If we cannot do so, then we cannot be sure the revelation is a genuine revelation.

This line of reasoning seems fallacious to me. If it were correct, then it would be impossible in general for rational beings of limited powers to recognise the superiority of other beings, but this is something that human beings do all the time. The fallacy lies in the assumption that the only way of determining the cognitive superiority of another being would be by coming to know independently what that being knows. It does seem that one way of coming to recognise the superiority of another being would be to verify for oneself what the superior being claims to know. But even in this case the superiority of the other being might be evident in the greater ease or certainty of knowing or the reliability of the knowledge which the superior being manifests. However, there are a number of other possibilities as to how one might recognise the superiority of another cognitive agent. Some of these can be seen if we think about the hypothetical case of an extra-terrestrial intelligent being.

First, such a being might show knowledge about things that we have knowledge about, but gain that knowledge in a way that manifests powers we do not possess. This might sometimes hinge on the time or place at which something is known. I know what I ate for breakfast this morning because I remember it. If I met a being who was not around to observe what I ate for breakfast but could reliably tell me what I ate, I would have to conclude that this being had ways of discovering truths that I do not have. A similar case would be that of a being who exhibited foreknowledge. Imagine a being who knows exactly what the weather will be like the following day. After the fact I might have the same knowledge, but the fact that another being had knowledge of some fact before its occurrence could be strong evidence of superior power.

Secondly, a being might give evidence of superior cognitive powers by showing that the being had other kinds of superior powers, such as technological power. For example, if I met a being who had the power to transport itself from one place to another instantaneously without any visible mechanism, I should certainly conclude that this being is superior to me in technological power, and it seems reasonable to infer that such technological power would be accompanied by, perhaps would even require, greater cognitive power as well.

Of course to believe the testimony of some extra-terrestrial being, I would doubtless require more than simply a belief in the cognitive superiority of the being. I would also need a belief that the being in question intended to tell me the truth, rather than deceive me, and this belief might in turn require some beliefs about the character of the being in question. Whether I would need some positive evidence for this belief or whether it would be reasonable to believe in the good intentions of the being unless I had reason to doubt (as some versions of what is called 'the principle of credulity' might imply) I shall leave an open question.

In any case it appears to me that the criteria Aquinas gives for recognising a revelation as one that ought to be believed because it comes from God (or angels perhaps) are roughly parallel to the ways we might come to recognise the superiority of an extra-terrestrial being and come to accept the testimony of that being. Aquinas says we can come to see the genuineness of the revelation partly by confirming some of the truths contained in it for ourselves. Even in these cases the superiority of the revealer can be shown by the certainty and the manner in which these truths are known. But a crucial factor for Aquinas is the miracles that should accompany a genuine revelation, because these provide evidence that the revelation does indeed come from a being whose powers exceed those of any being known in the natural world. Presumably the character and intentions of the revealer can also be known in some way, both from the nature of the revelation itself and from the character of the accompanying miracles. Fideism, insofar as it consists of the claim that human reason should be willing to recognise its limits and believe what it can learn from a being of superior powers, seems in principle a reasonable position.

NOTES

1. Thomas Aquinas, *Summa Theologiae* I, 12, 4. Translation is taken from the *Basic Writings of Thomas Aquinas*, ed. Anton C. Pegis (New York: Random House, 1945) p. 97. References to the first volume of the *Summa Theologiae* (ST I) will be from this edition, unless otherwise noted.
2. Thomas Aquinas, *Summa Theologiae* I, 12, 11. This particular translation is taken from the Image Books edition, Gen. ed. Thomas Gilby (Garden City, New York: Doubleday and Company, 1969) p. 189. The corresponding translation from the Pegis edition (*Basic Writings of Thomas Aquinas*) is on p. 107. In this case I find the Pegis translation somewhat misleading.
3. Thomas Aquinas, *Summa Contra Gentiles* I, 14, 2–3, trans. Anton C. Pegis (Notre Dame, Indiana: University of Notre Dame Press, 1975) pp. 96–7, gives a clear account of the use of negative terms to describe God. Bk I, Chp. 34 discusses analogy. All references to *Summa Contra Gentiles* (SCG) will be from this edition. The corresponding section in the *Summa Theologiae* is in Bk I, Qn 13.
4. Thomas Aquinas, SCG I, 3, 2 (p. 63).
5. Ibid.
6. See ST Bk I, Qn 46, articles 2 and 3, for Aquinas' argument that the fact that the world had a beginning in time is knowable only by revealed faith. From the point of view of reason it is equally rational to believe that the world has always existed.
7. SCG, I, Chps 15–22 (pp. 98–120).
8. ST I, 32, 1 (pp. 315–18).
9. ST I, 12, 13 (p. 111). The Image Books edition translates this as a 'sort of knowledge' (p. 194).
10. SCG I, 3, 3 (p. 64).
11. SCG, I, 4, 1 (p. 66).
12. SCG I, 8, 1 (p. 76).
13. Ibid
14. Aquinas distinguishes between the inward act of faith, which is to 'think with assent', and the 'outward act of faith', which is confession. See *Summa Theologiae*, 2–2, 2, A. 1, trans. Mark D. Jordan (Notre Dame, Indiana: University of Notre Dame Press, 1990) pp. 65–8, and ST 2–2, 3, A. 1, pp. 95–6. All references to ST II will be from this edition.
15. ST 2–2, 2, 2 (pp. 69–70).
16. SCG I, 6, 1 (p. 71).
17. SCG I, 6, 1 (pp. 71–72).
18. SCG I, 6, 4 (p. 73).
19. ST 2–2, 2, 10 (p. 90).
20. SCG I, 5, 5 (p. 71).
21. SCG I, 5, 2 (p. 69).
22. SCG I, 5, 3 (p. 70).
23. SCG I, 5, 4 (p. 70).
24. SCG I, 3, 4 (p. 65).

5

Faith Above Reason: Kant

One form that responsible fideism takes is the claim that faith requires beliefs that are above reason. However, this claim that there are propositions that are above reason that should be believed by faith can itself be interpreted in several senses. In the last chapter I examined Aquinas as a representative of the view that there are some revealed propositions that must be believed even though reason cannot by itself determine their truth. Such a view is consistent with the possibility that reason could discover arguments or evidence that bear on these truths, even if not conclusively. However, it is possible to hold that there are propositions proposed as beliefs to be held by faith that cannot even be investigated by reason.

One could of course consider this simply a special case of the kind of view Aquinas holds. One way that reason might fail to be competent to determine the truth of a belief would be the case where reason cannot investigate the belief at all. Nevertheless, this case is special enough to warrant some consideration in its own right. I should like to examine some of Immanuel Kant's claims about the relation between theoretical reason and the existence of God as an example of this kind of fideism. I shall interpret Kant as arguing that there are some truths that reason, in its theoretical employment, can say nothing about, but which can and should be accepted by faith.

As we shall see, faith is for Kant also connected with reason. Specifically, faith is linked to reason in its practical employment, reason insofar as it is directed to deciding what to do. Since faith is rational for Kant, one might argue that it is a mistake to classify Kant as a fideist. However, Kant himself consistently contrasts faith with *knowledge*, which is something gained through theoretical reason. The sharp limits Kant wishes to put upon knowledge, and the way in which he sees faith as linked to action rather than theoretical insight, are themes that stamp Kant as at least strongly influenced by fideism. The fact that he argues that faith in this sense is rational is not by itself enough to rule out the application of the term 'fideism' to Kant, unless we want to make responsible fideism impossible by definition.

Kant's general project with respect to religious knowledge is memorably summed up in his own Preface to the second edition of the *Critique of Pure Reason*: 'I have therefore found it necessary to deny *knowledge*, in order to make room for *faith*'.[1] Kant believes that true religion is best served by the critical destruction of dogmatic philosophical foundations; by removing spurious claims to religious knowledge, the true character of religious faith can emerge more clearly. So there is a clear fideistic thrust to Kant's work. The question of whether or not Kant is or is not a fideist is probably not a useful one in the final analysis. Rather, just as was the case with Aquinas, my goal will be to explore what might be called fideistic themes or elements in Kant's thought. By pursuing this course we may be able to clarify the different senses of 'fideism' and decide whether or not Kant was in some sense a fideist.

One particular fideistic theme in Kant that is worth investigating is his view that, from the viewpoint of theoretical reason, truths about God are 'transcendent'. They are, in a strict sense, above theoretical reason and reason can neither affirm them nor deny them.

It will be helpful to digress just a bit at this point and say something about how Kant uses the term 'reason', though I will say more about this later. As I have already implied, Kant distinguishes between theoretical and practical reason. They are not, however, two different faculties of reason. Rather, Kant thinks of reason as a single faculty having two different uses. Specifically, reason is employed theoretically, to gain knowledge of the world, and practically, to decide what actions in that world to perform. When Kant speaks about 'reason' in an unqualified manner, however, he usually has theoretical reason in mind, and I shall follow his terminological practice. Even within the theoretical sphere, there is an ambiguity. Kant sometimes uses the term 'reason' for the whole of the theoretical sphere, and sometimes uses it for a specialised part of the process of theoretical inquiry. I will say more about this narrower concept of theoretical reason below.

There are some noted differences between Kant's version of 'faith as believing what is above reason' and the view of Aquinas examined in the last chapter. First and most obvious is a difference in the content of what is said to be above reason. For Aquinas, there are many important truths about God that must be accepted by faith, but the existence of God and many other truths about God can be known by reason. For Kant, however, all *knowledge* of God is above reason.

Second, and equally important, is a difference in how faith is conceived. While Aquinas sees faith as rational, its essence is an acceptance of some historically revealed truth because of one's judgment as to the trustworthiness of the revealer. Thus faith is necessarily linked to a special revelation. For Kant, however, the kind of faith in which he is most interested is grounded in what he terms pure practical reason, which is reasoning about what a person ought morally to do. Faith is rational because it is linked to the moral life. While Kant certainly does not rule out the possibility of an historical revelation and does not claim that it is necessarily irrational to believe in such a revelation, he does argue for the possibility of a pure moral faith that is not tied to such a revelation.[2] More historical kinds of faith that are tied to particular churches must, according to Kant, have this pure moral faith as their highest interpreter.[3]

KANT'S ACCOUNT OF KNOWLEDGE

It is difficult briefly to summarise Kant's complex theory of human knowledge, but to understand his views about religious knowledge, some basic review is necessary. In a famous sentence, Kant held that 'though all our knowledge begins with experience, it does not follow that it all arises out of experience'.[4] It is crucial to Kant's philosophy to affirm that not all of our concepts are empirical, empirical ones being those such as our concepts of 'dog' or 'red'. That is, not all human concepts are derived simply from our sense experiences; some must be *a priori.* This neat distinction between empirical and *a priori* concepts is one that is problematic in light of recent philosophical arguments, and I will later raise some questions about it, but Kant himself has no doubts that this distinction can be sharply drawn.

Among the non-empirical or *a priori* concepts there are what Kant calls the 'categories of the understanding'. Kant distinguishes the 'understanding', which is the faculty that forms judgments, from 'reason' in the strict sense, which is the ability to make inferences. Reason in this limited sense is the source of *a priori* concepts too, to be discussed below. The *a priori* categories of the understanding for Kant are crucial for scientific knowledge. When we move from merely receiving sense impressions to forming judgments about what we have experienced, we necessarily employ such categories of the understanding as 'cause' and 'substance'.

These categories represent the way the human understanding necessarily functions. For Kant this means we can, for example, know with certainty that whatever we experience we will understand as linked by the relations of cause and effect, and that we do have knowledge of a world of substances or permanent objects. We can know this in the same way we could know that the picture on a black and white television set can only represent black and white and shades of grey; the structure of the television guarantees that it is so. The categories represent the structure of what we might call the 'receiving apparatus' of our own minds and we can therefore know *a priori* that what we know will conform to that structure.

Of course, just because I have a black and white television, it does not follow that all the things I see on my television are really black and white. Many of the things I see on television are in reality coloured. In a similar manner, Kant argues that our human knowledge is not knowledge of reality as it is in itself; it is only knowledge of reality as it appears to us. The categories are objective in the sense of being the same for all humans on his view (another questionable claim) and give us genuine knowledge, but it is a knowledge of appearances. We have no guarantee that reality in itself must conform to the categories of the human understanding.

Kant thinks he has thereby shown that scientific knowledge, which is based on experience and presupposes the categories of the understanding, is legitimate, but it is not *metaphysical* knowledge. In his terminology, science gives us knowledge of phenomena or appearances but no knowledge of noumena, or things in themselves. However, Kant does not think that this settles the question of whether any metaphysical knowledge is possible for human beings.

METAPHYSICS AND THE IDEA OF GOD

Kant thinks that we humans are necessarily interested in metaphysics. We have, for example, an abiding interest in questions about God and immortality. As he puts it, we cannot ignore these metaphysical questions, but curiously enough, it turns out we cannot answer them either.[5] Metaphysical questions are raised when we consider what Kant calls the Ideas of pure reason. These Ideas are not categories that apply to possible experiences, but are Ideas of that which transcends any possible sense experience in this life. We cannot develop a concept of God as a possible object of experience, according to Kant, but we necessarily develop an Idea of God nevertheless.

How does this Idea develop? According to Kant, the Idea of God that theoretical reason develops is derived from the need of reason to explain the facts discovered by the understanding. We explain by showing how some fact or principle can be derived from some more fundamental 'condition'. There is an inner infinity to this process, in that whatever explanation is given can in principle be subsumed under a yet more fundamental explanation. This restless striving could only be fulfilled by some kind of ultimate explanation, the Idea of an Unconditioned Condition.[6] Such an explanation would explain everything else while itself requiring no explanation. Essentially, then, for Kant, theoretical reason thinks of God as the Ultimate Reason for everything, the First Cause or Final Explanation.

Kant thinks that reason has a curiously ambivalent relation to this Idea of reason. On the one hand, reason needs to think of reality as ultimately intelligible and thus needs to approach its task with the assumption that there is some ultimate explanation of everything; reason at least must not think reality is ultimately unintelligible. The Idea of God thus has an important 'regulative' or guiding role for theoretical reason. However, Kant thinks that both reason and religion would be harmed by actual knowledge of God. Religion would be harmed because if God were known, then God would necessarily be part of the spatio-temporal world to which the categories of the understanding are always applied, and thus God's transcendence would be compromised. Reason would be harmed because if God were actually known, then human beings would 'appeal directly to the unsearchable decrees of divine wisdom' to explain the world, rather than seeking to discover 'causes in the universal laws of material mechanism'.[7] Essentially, Kant wants to hold that thinking of the world as grounded in God is desirable for science, but one must not appeal to God as a substitute for concrete scientific explanation.

In a strong sense, then, an Idea of reason, such as the Idea of God, marks the boundary or limit of reason. The Idea of God is meaningful to reason; it is an Idea that reason must think. However, it an Idea that can never become an object of knowledge. Kant thinks there is a strong, even 'natural', tendency for reason to be deceived by an illusion at this point; reason tends to move from its own need to think about the world in terms of God to the conclusion that God's existence is an objective necessity. Kant seems to be somewhat ambivalent about this 'illusion'. On the one hand, he sees it as the source of rationalistic metaphysics, an attitude of dogmatism that Kant's own 'critical' philosophy is supposed to dispel. The mistake occurs when we 'take the subjective necessity of a connection of our concepts, which is to the advantage of the understanding, for an objective necessity in the determination of things in themselves'.[8] In other words, reason is seen as making a mistake, and it is Kant's philosophy that is supposed to reveal the mistake.

However, the illusion is, on Kant's view, not a mere mistake or blunder, because it is grounded in the very nature of reason, the need of reason to think of the world as finally intelligible. The illusion is in some sense 'natural' or even 'inevitable', an illusion 'which can no more be prevented than we can prevent the sea appearing higher at the horizon than at the shore'.[9] Kant clearly does not mean the illusion is inevitable in the sense that we cannot help making the mistake in question; he must mean rather that there is something in the nature of reason itself that always tempts us to make a certain kind of mistake.[10] Presumably, when we recognise the limits of reason we do not make this mistake.

But how can reason recognise its own limits? Must not reason transcend those limits in order to recognise them? As Wittgenstein says, 'in order to be able to set a limit to thought, we should have to find both sides of the limit thinkable (i.e. we should have to be able to think what cannot be thought)'.[11] Part of Kant's answer to this difficulty is the analysis he has given of knowledge. If all human knowledge presupposes the application of the categories, and if the categories of the understanding can only be applied to what could conceivably be experienced by the senses in space and time, then we can know *a priori* that an Idea that reason must consider but that cannot be experienced by the senses in a spatio-temporal manner falls outside the limits of human knowledge.

A crucial clue that reason has encountered its limit is found in what Kant calls the antinomies of pure reason.[12] Kant argues that when reason does try to gain knowledge about the Ideas, it falls into apparent contradictions. These contradictions, or antinomies, are created when reason attempts to conceive of the world as a whole as a completed totality that can be explained. Kant claims that reason can offer proofs that have the appearance of logical soundness for a number of contradictory propositions. Reason can, for example, construct arguments for the claim that the world is limited in time and space, but also for the claim that the world is infinite in time and space. Most relevantly for our subject, reason can put forward arguments designed to show both that a necessary being (God) must exist either as part of or cause of the universe and also that no such being exists.[13] This conflict of reason with itself is seen by Kant as a sign that reason has trespassed beyond its proper boundaries. The cure requires reason to recognise that the boundaries of knowledge extend only to the limits of the realm of appearances and not to things in themselves.

The Idea of God is then for Kant 'above reason' in a quite strict sense. Reason can and must think the Idea but cannot claim to know its object. Nevertheless, Kant argues that the Idea is one that can be rationally embraced – through moral faith. The critical philosopher must 'subdue the rashness and presumption of those who so far misconstrue the true vocation of reason as to boast of insight and knowledge just where true insight and knowledge cease'.[14] However, the critical philosopher should not cut humans off 'from employing intellectual *presuppositions* and *faith* on behalf of our practical interest'.[15] Such faith is legitimate so long as it does not pretend to be knowledge.

MORAL FAITH AS THE GROUND OF BELIEF IN GOD

A full statement of how Kant views religious faith and grounds it in morality is beyond the scope of this chapter.[16] However, a brief sketch will give some idea as to how he thinks it is possible for an individual to believe what is above reason. Kant's general moral theory is well known; he holds that what makes an act morally right is not the results intended or achieved by the act, but rather the maxim, or subjective principle, on which the act is based. The maxims themselves must be selected, if actions are to be moral, on the basis of what Kant calls the 'categorical imperative', the supreme principle of morality: 'Act only according to that maxim whereby you can at the same time will that it should become a universal law'.[17]

Kant sees this principle as binding on all rational beings, although a being that was perfectly rational would not experience it as an imperative or command, since such a being would naturally act in accord with it.[18] The principle is rational because it embodies the demand of reason for coherence and consistency. The essence of immorality becomes inconsistency, making an exception in your own case to those principles that are recognised as generally binding.

Thus for Kant morality is not determined by any consideration of consequences but solely by the principles on which actions are to be based. Nevertheless, all concrete actions do aim at consequences. Though my act does not have to be determined by the end I seek, to act is necessarily to seek some end that is perceived as good. For Kant, the comprehensive and complete end of moral action would be what he terms the highest good. What is the good that moral agents seek? Put briefly, it is a world where people are both morally virtuous and happy.

The only absolute and unqualified good for Kant is a morally good will – the possession of a virtuous character. Without moral character, other goods such as intelligence can be perverted. Nevertheless, there are many other goods that human beings desire, and a morally good person pursues those goods – both for himself and others. The sum total of all these 'natural' goods for Kant is happiness, a condition where everything goes according to one's will. Thus the highest good can be briefly described as a world where people are supremely morally virtuous and happy, with that happiness contingent upon virtue.

Thus, when I act morally it is the highest good in this sense that I seek to realise. Nevertheless, I am not allowed to cut any moral corners in seeking to realise this good; the highest good cannot be detached from morality as a goal that could be achieved by immoral means. Can I hope to make any progress towards the realisation of this goal? As Kant sees it, if God exists and is the author of the physical world with its physical laws, then such hope is rational. For in that case I have reason to think that the causal laws by which results in the physical world are achieved are governed by a moral providence.

Put bluntly, if God does not exist and the universe is simply a physical machine with no moral purposiveness at work within it, then human beings have no reason to think that moral action can be effective in bringing about the highest good that includes happiness. In Kant's words, if God does not exist, then there is 'an open contradiction' between 'a final end within, that is set before them [human beings] as a duty, and a nature without, that has no final end, though in it the former end is to be actualized'.[19] If the moral agent is to see moral action as efficacious, he or she must regard the natural world as an arena for moral endeavour, a theatre where moral striving can be effective, which in turn requires the agent to see nature as permeated by a moral purposiveness. Action for an end is irrational unless that end is at least one that it is possible to achieve. I cannot try to bring about a result that I know is impossible. The end of morality is a goal that reason itself lays upon rational beings; in seeking to be moral, I necessarily seek the highest good, and I must therefore believe that the natural world is governed in such a way that this good is in fact attainable.

To summarise the argument briefly, for Kant what I ought to do I must believe is possible for me to do: ought implies can. I ought to seek the highest good. I cannot try to achieve an end if I believe that it is not possible for me to realise that end, or at least to make progress towards doing so. The highest good is not attainable if God does not exist as the ultimate governing power of the world. Therefore I must believe in God's reality.[20]

IS KANT'S VIEW DEFENSIBLE?

For Kant belief in God is not knowledge, but faith, because it is not grounded in theoretical insight concerning the character of the world. The Idea of the ground of the natural world cannot be transformed into knowledge because it is above reason. Nevertheless, it is an Idea which theoretical reason provides to practical reason, and the moral faith that arises out of practical reason is a rational faith.

How much of Kant's philosophy of religion remains defensible? It is clear that Kant's views about God are closely linked to elements in his philosophy that are by no means uncontroversial. Some of his claims appear dubious indeed. Kant's philosophy is standardly viewed as an attempted synthesis between two types of modern philosophy: rationalism and empiricism. This is correct, but I shall claim that Kant incorporates elements from both empiricism and rationalism that are hard to defend. Nevertheless, I shall argue that despite these problems elements in Kant's approach remain promising.

One of the dubious elements in Kant's philosophy is the sharp distinction he draws between the empirical and the non-empirical. Kant tells us that he was awakened from his rationalistic 'dogmatic slumbers' by reading empiricist David Hume, but it can be argued that when Kant read Hume he simply substituted one set of dogmas for another. In particular, he seems to have accepted uncritically the empiricist claim that human knowledge is limited to sense experience. The difficulty is that the concept of 'sense experience' is not itself a clear one. The history of empiricism, particularly the so-called 'logical positivists' and 'logical empiricists' of the twentieth century, shows that no one has successfully shown how the concepts necessary for science can all be derived from sense experience.[21]

One might think that this result is a vindication for Kant, since he agrees with rationalists that science depends on *a priori* as well as empirical concepts. However, Kant's treatment of the *a priori* depends on a sharp distinction between empirical and *a priori* concepts, a distinction that turns out to be very difficult to draw. A strong case has been made in recent philosophy of science that scientific theories require concepts of unobservable 'theoretical' objects.[22] Such concepts are not *a priori* but they are not strictly empirical in Kant's sense either.

Such theoretical concepts appear to undermine one of Kant's reasons for denying that knowledge of God is possible, for they imply that the fact that an object cannot be directly experienced is no barrier to gaining knowledge about that object. Scientists know a lot about many objects, such as black holes, that cannot be directly observed. It appears that Kant's major objection to knowledge of God is that such knowledge would imply that God is a 'sensible object', since he requires that knowledge be knowledge of objects that are at least temporal (in the case of psychological or mental entities) or spatio-temporal (in the case of external objects), and space and time for Kant are the 'forms of intuition'. That is, space and time are features of the way we organise our experience rather than features of what we experience. However, Kant's view that space and time are universal *a priori* concepts that have no application to reality looks dubious in light of the transformations these concepts have undergone in contemporary physics. We may not know that God is temporal, for example, but we may not know that he is not either. In any case, it does not follow that we must think of God as a *part* of the temporal world if we think of him as the cause of that world. In fact, Kant himself really must admit this insofar as he claims that we do have an *Idea* of God.

A number of contemporary writers have attempted to show that Kantian-style objections to rational arguments for God are not decisive, since the concept of God can figure in explanations of the existence of the world or of certain features of the world, and such explanations are at least analogous to ordinary scientific 'inferences to the best explanation'.[23] Whether these kinds of arguments succeed or not, Kant's claim that they cannot succeed because they attempt to extend knowledge beyond the bounds of experience appears to rest on discredited empiricist dogma.

Kant would doubtless have found this type of attempted justification of religious belief unacceptable for yet another reason, but a look at this reason highlights yet another problem area in Kant's thought. This other element in Kant stems from his rationalism. Like his rationalist forebears, Kant thinks that genuine knowledge must be 'apodictic' or completely certain. He thinks that philosophy must be a 'rigorous science' and that a real science must reach conclusions that are known with absolute certainty. In fact, though Kant thinks that rationalistic metaphysics is a kind of immodest attempt to overstep the bounds of reason, he is not very modest about his own critical, rational enterprise. He says, rather, that in dealing with 'pure reason' we should be able to resolve all questions once and for all.[24]

Now the kind of rational arguments for God's existence put forward today by such thinkers as Richard Swinburne do not claim absolute certainty in this way. Hence for Kant such arguments simply fail as rigorous philosophy. An argument that does not lead to absolute certainty simply has no value at all.

However, in this dispute it is surely Kant's conception of philosophy and science that is defective. In the natural sciences, contrary to Kant's own assumption that Newtonian science represented some kind of final truth, it is generally recognised that even well-confirmed theories can be overthrown, and hardly any philosophers would wish to claim that philosophy, whether speculative or critical, can be final in the way that Kant thought. So, once again, the fact that rational arguments for God's existence do not lead to certain, final knowledge hardly gives us a reason to regard these arguments as philosophically worthless. Kant, while rejecting the conclusions of rationalistic metaphysics, still accepts its understanding of the nature of philosophy and the standards that must be met for genuine knowledge.[25]

However, despite these weaknesses, I think there are insights in Kant's approach that are still defensible. Kant's own argument that God's transcendence blocks any knowledge of God may rest on discredited empiricist dogmas, but there are religious reasons for maintaining something like Kant's view, and these reasons are independent of empiricism. It was a deep conviction of the ancient Hebrews that no mortal can 'see' God and live.[26] It is this conviction that lies behind the view of Aquinas, discussed in the last chapter, that no mortal can clearly conceive God's essence in this life. Such a religious doctrine of transcendence may not lead to an absolute barrier to any meaningful talk about God or knowledge of God; at least it did not do so for Aquinas. Rather, as we saw, Aquinas allows for a kind of 'relational' knowledge of God, in which, though we lack knowledge of God's own essence, we can know something about God under various descriptions. We can, for example, know God as the creator of the universe, the 'first cause' of all change.

So if Kant's aversion to theoretical knowledge of God is grounded in a religious concept of transcendence rather than empiricist strictures that limit knowledge to what can be experienced with the senses, that aversion may have to be, like that of Aquinas, more nuanced and less absolute in character. If we give up the rationalist demand that philosophy lead to conclusions that are apodictically certain, then there seems to be no reason to think it would be necessarily illegitimate to think of God as the cause of the existence of the universe or its orderliness or goodness. Kant's own view to the contrary depends on his claim that a concept like 'cause' is an *a priori* one that can legitimately be applied only within the supposedly clear realm of sensible experience. If we have no principled way of specifying what that realm is, then Kant's claim that the categories cannot be legitimately applied to God seems unproven.

However, though theoretical attempts to justify belief in God or some beliefs about God may be legitimate, if God is truly infinite in the way that the great monotheistic religions have always claimed, then there may still be much about God that exceeds human rational capacities. Humans may be capable of some true beliefs about God, but a genuine understanding of who God is may be quite impossible for theoretical reason.

Even the limited kind of theoretical knowledge about God that might be possible may be dubious for another reason that Kant has a sure grasp upon. The heart of Kant's philosophy of religion is his insistence that the knowledge of God is *practical* in character. The discovery of God's reality is not like the discovery of the neutrino or some other exotic sub-atomic particle. Such discoveries in physics may be exciting to physicists, but they have no direct bearing on what we might call the human task, those obligations and duties that are binding on all human persons. Knowing God, however, is supposed to make a difference to how people view themselves and their task. The link with action is twofold. On the one hand, knowing God has implications for how we are to live. It is also true that to know God we may have to possess particular moral and spiritual qualities. We come to know God, not simply by being intellectually acute or scientifically knowledgeable, but by coming to know ourselves and by becoming a certain kind of person, one with the right kinds of moral and spiritual virtues.

Once more Kant's thought here is linked to a deep strand within the tradition. Within Christianity, at least, *faith* has long been held to be a necessary condition for knowing God, or at least for attaining an adequate or deep knowledge of him. Faith here is surely not a name for merely believing without evidence, though it may include that. Faith is a name for those moral and spiritual qualities that give the individual the capacity to know God. Kant's conception of faith is arguably one-sided in putting so much emphasis on morality as the key to the knowledge of God. We shall see in the next chapter that Kierkegaard, for one, does not think faith can be reduced to the moral life in the way Kant tries to do. However, Kant's instincts in linking religiously significant knowledge of God to practical life more than to scientific theory seem right to me.

It is not that Kant rules out any role for theoretical reason. Even with his own rationalistic constraints, he sees that the perspective of theoretical reason is important to the faith of practical reason. It is vital that we have a concept of the ultimate ground of the universe, the Unconditioned Condition, that moral faith can appropriate and infuse with moral content. However, it is just as vital for him that this Idea of Theoretical Reason should not be an item of knowledge. As we have seen, this can be viewed as a way of trying to secure God's transcendence. Kant also thinks that if God were merely an object of theoretical knowledge, the character of the knower would be irrelevant to whether the knowledge could be obtained. Insofar as awareness of God is grounded in moral faith, the apprehension of God is linked to the moral character of the knower. For Kant, then, apprehending God by faith is not a 'second-best' substitute for theoretical knowledge, but the most appropriate way in which religious insights could be had. It is precisely the fact that religious truths are above reason that allows us to become aware of a transcendent God and to be morally transformed ourselves in the process of becoming aware of God.

NOTES

1. Immanuel Kant, *Critique of Pure Reason*, trans. Norman Kemp Smith (New York: St Martins Press, 1965) p. 29.
2. See Immanuel Kant, *Religion Within the Limits of Reason Alone*, trans. Theodore M. Greene and Hoyt H. Hudson (New York: Harper and Row, 1960) pp. 94–100.
3. Kant, *Religion Within the Limits of Reason Alone*, pp. 100–5.
4. Kant, *Critique of Pure Reason*, p. 41.
5. Kant, *Critique of Pure Reason*, p. 7.
6. Kant, *Critique of Pure Reason*, p. 316.
7. Kant, *Critique of Pure Reason*, p. 562.
8. Kant, *Critique of Pure Reason*, p. 299.
9. Ibid.
10. Kant, *Critique of Pure Reason*, p. 300.
11. Ludwig Wittgenstein, *Tractatus Logico-Philosophicus* (London: Routledge and Kegan Paul, 1961) p. 3.
12. Kant's long discussion of the 'Antinomy of Pure Reason' is found in the *Critique of Pure Reason*, Bk II, Chp. II of the 'Transcendental Dialectic' section (pp. 384–484 in the Kemp Smith translation).
13. Kant, *Critique of Pure Reason*, pp. 415–21.
14. Kant, *Critique of Pure Reason*, p. 427.
15. Ibid.
16. A fuller statement from the present author can be found in *Subjectivity and Religious Belief: An Historical, Critical Study* (Grand Rapids, Michigan: Wm B. Eerdmans, 1978), Chp. 2. Allen Wood's *Kant's Moral Religion* (Ithaca, New York: Cornell University Press, 1970) is a fine, book-length study.
17. Immanuel Kant, *Grounding for the Metaphysics of Morals*, 3rd edn trans. James Ellington (Indianapolis, Indiana: Hackett Publishing Co., 1993) p. 30.
18. See Kant, *Grounding for the Metaphysics of Morals*, p. 24.
19. Immanuel Kant, *Critique of Judgment*, trans. James Meredith (Oxford: Oxford University Press, 1952) p. 129.
20. Strictly speaking, one might think that Kant's argument only justifies belief that God's existence is possible, and Kant in fact does at one point admit that this is the minimum that moral faith demands. However, he clearly thinks that a more robust faith is more conducive to a more robust form of the moral life. For a clear discussion of this point, see Allen Wood, *Kant's Moral Religion* (Ithaca, New York: Cornell University Press, 1970) p. 31.
21. For a classic article that explores some of the difficulties, see Carl Hempel, 'Problems and Changes in the Empiricist Criterion of Meaning', in *Revue Internationale de Philosophie* (IV, 11; January 15, 1950); reprinted in *Classics of Analytic Philosophy*, ed. Robert Ammerman (Indianapolis, Indiana: Hackett Publishing Co., 1990) pp. 214–30.
22. For a good introductory treatment, see Del Ratzsch, *Philosophy of Science: The Natural Sciences in Christian Perspective* (Downers Grove, Illinois: InterVarsity Press, 1986), particularly chapters 2 and 3, which discuss the revolt of Thomas Kuhn and others against empiricist philosophy of science, as well as the contemporary situation.
23. Probably the best-known example of this kind of argument is found in Richard Swinburne, *The Existence of God* (Oxford: Oxford University Press, 1979) and also *Is There a God?* (Oxford: Oxford University Press, 1996). Also see Michael Banner, *The Justification of Science and the Rationality of Religious Belief* (Oxford: Oxford University Press, 1990).
24. Kant, *Critique of Pure Reason*, p. 10.
25. See F. E. England's argument that Kant, 'while rejecting the content of Wolffian metaphysics [Christian Wolff], still conforms to its method'. *Kant's Conception of God* (London: George Allen and Unwin, 1929) pp. 180–1.
26. For a story that expresses this insight in a very curious manner, see the account, found in Exodus 33:17–23, of God's appearance to Moses, in which Moses asks to see God's face. God informs Moses that he cannot do this and live, but still passes before Moses, covering Moses' face so that Moses can live, but then allowing Moses a glimpse of God's back.

6

Faith Above Reason: Kierkegaard

Søren Kierkegaard is often cited in textbooks as a prime example of irrational fideism. Many would say that Kierkegaard, unlike Aquinas and Kant, is a true fideist, and in his works we see a repudiation of reason. I am convinced that this reading is mistaken, and that Kierkegaard is best understood as a responsible fideist. Part of my reason for discussing Aquinas and Kant is to show similarities between their thinking and Kierkegaard. If elements of their thinking can be viewed as responsible fideism, perhaps Kierkegaard can be viewed this way as well. However, it is true that Kierkegaard holds more radical views than Aquinas and Kant. As we shall see, Kierkegaard seems to assert fideism in two different senses; he claims, as did Aquinas and Kant, that faith is above reason, though he understands this claim somewhat differently from how they did. However, he also asserts that faith must be understood as *against* reason. In this chapter, I shall look at Kierkegaard's understanding of faith as above reason, completing my analysis of that form of fideism. In the next chapter I shall examine Kierkegaard's claim that faith is in tension with or opposition to reason. In both cases, however, I will argue that Kierkegaard is a responsible fideist. His writings show an awareness of the limits of reason and the ability of reason to become self-critical, but they do not imply any repudiation of reason.

Before beginning a serious discussion of Kierkegaard's views there is one interpretive problem that must be faced. Many of Kierkegaard's writings are attributed by Kierkegaard himself to various pseudonyms. These pseudonyms should be taken seriously, since they are for Kierkegaard like characters in a novel, who may therefore have views that are not shared by their author. Hence it is not always clear what passages in Kierkegaard's writings represent his own viewpoints. In scholarly work whose primary purpose is to exposit Kierkegaard, it is very important to distinguish Kierkegaard from those pseudonyms. However, in most textbooks this distinction is not observed, and the views often attributed to 'Kierkegaard' are taken from one or more of the pseudonymous 'characters'. In this book my primary purpose is to examine a position taken in some of Kierkegaard's writings, a position that is usually identified as Kierkegaard's own view. Hence, to avoid complexity in the exposition that might create needless confusion, I shall here follow the textbook practice and speak of 'Kierkegaard' as the author of the pseudonymous works. I do think the position I shall attribute to Kierkegaard corresponds to his actual views, but to show this in detail would require a complicated analysis of the various pseudonyms and their relation to Kierkegaard.[1]

THE INCARNATION AND KANT'S IDEA OF REASON

In Chapter 4 we looked at Aquinas' claim that faith involves belief in propositions that are above reason in the sense that their truth cannot be determined by reason. In Chapter 5 we looked at Kant's more radical proposal that what he calls the Ideas of reason (including the Idea of God) lie completely beyond the boundaries of reason, even though they can and should be accepted by faith, a faith that is linked to practical reason but not based on theoretical knowledge. Kant, however, insists that the Idea of God can and must be *thought* by reason. Though he does say that we have no *concept* of God, this is because for Kant a concept is a concept of something that could only be experienced in space and time, and God is not a spatio-temporal object.[2] The overall thrust of Kant's view is clearly that God can be thought but not known by theoretical reason.

It is, I believe, illuminating to compare Kierkegaard's thoughts on this issue of the proper object of faith with both Aquinas and Kant. Like Aquinas, Kierkegaard thinks the beliefs that are above reason and therefore properly objects of faith to be specifically Christian beliefs derived from revelation, rather than merely being a general belief in God. (As we shall see there are also differences between Kierkegaard and Aquinas in how these revealed truths appear to us and how they are to be accepted.) Though Kant does not rule out faith in a revelation with historical content, the essential kind of faith for him is a pure moral faith in God. In Kierkegaard's writings, the crucial object of faith, at least for the Christian believer, is not simply faith in God. At times he denies that belief in God should even be called 'faith', since it lacks the uncertainty of genuine faith. So, for example, in *Philosophical Fragments* he says that 'one does not have *faith* that the god exists, eternally understood, even though one assumes that the god exists. That is improper use of language. Socrates did not have faith that the god existed.'[3] At other times he admits that belief in God does require something like faith, since proofs of God's existence are never decisive, and in fact require faith to be accepted.[4] In fact, in *Concluding Unscientific Postscript* he admits there is a kind of 'Socratic' faith in God that is possible for humans generally, and says that *Fragments* was in error in denying that Socrates had faith.[5] However, even though he admits there is something like generic faith in God, the kind of faith that he is most concerned about is faith in the God-in-time, the God who has become incarnate as a human person in history.

So there is a crucial difference in the content of faith between Kant and Kierkegaard. Nevertheless, there are some striking parallels between Kant's Idea of God and Kierkegaard's concept of the God-in-time.[6] Kierkegaard sees the incarnation as the boundary or limit of reason in much the same way that Kant saw the Idea of God, something that reason is driven to try and think but cannot comprehend.[7] For Kierkegaard the attempt to comprehend the incarnation results in 'contradictions', a view that seems formally parallel to Kant's view that when reason tries to know the Ideas it falls into 'antinomies'.

Despite these parallels, there are significant differences between the functions of the Kierkegaardian idea of the God-in-time and the Kantian Idea of God. For Kant, though the Idea of God cannot be known by reason, it is in some sense a 'natural' idea of reason, one that plays a positive, regulative function in leading reason onward to higher and more comprehensive explanations. It is a concrete expression of reason's faith in the unity and intelligibility of the world. For Kierkegaard, however, the idea of the God-in-time is anything but 'natural'. He calls it the idea of the 'strangest of all things' and claims that it is an idea that could not have originated in any human being's thought.[8] Rather than being a natural thought of reason, it is the 'absolute paradox' and the 'absurd' to human reason.[9] Like Kant's Idea of Reason it is a boundary or limit of reason, 'that which thought cannot think'. However, it is a limit in a stronger sense. Here we have an Idea that not only falls outside the boundaries of knowledge, but in some sense resists being understood at all. It is above reason in a more radical sense of 'above'.

IS THE INCARNATION A LOGICAL CONTRADICTION?

How can faith believe what it cannot understand? Perhaps one can make sense of the idea that faith can believe what cannot be known, but it does not seem that faith can make what is unintelligible intelligible. This seems a sound point, and it implies that the unintelligibility of the paradox cannot be complete. When reason encounters the God-in-time, it must understand something, even to know that it has encountered what it cannot understand. However, we shall see that this requirement does not lessen the 'absoluteness' of the paradox for Kierkegaard.

Briefly put, the absolute paradox of the incarnation for Kierkegaard must be understood as the 'contradiction' that what is eternal (God) has nonetheless become temporal as a human being, so that existing human beings can come to know God and acquire eternal life by virtue of a relation to God in time.[10] 'In other words, because the eternal has come into existence at a moment of time, the existing individual in time does not come to relate himself to the eternal [i.e., does not do so eternally] . . . but *in time* comes to relate himself to the eternal *in time*'.[11] However, this formula can be more misleading than helpful unless we are careful to understand what Kierkegaard means by 'contradiction', 'eternity' and 'temporality'.

It is probably natural for contemporary readers to interpret 'contradiction' here as a formal, logical contradiction. On this reading, to say that the incarnation is a contradiction is simply to say that it is logically contradictory, like the positing of a square circle. The claim that a square is a circle is logically contradictory, since a square is necessarily non-circular; hence a square circle both is and is not a circle. Some interpreters of Kierkegaard read the notion of a 'God-man' as similar to the notion of a square circle.[12] Any claim that posits the existence of such a self-contradictory concept is necessarily false from the point of view of reason. On this reading, Kierkegaardian faith requires the sacrifice of the intellect, the suicide of reason. We have already examined fideism in this sense in Chapter 2 and found it wanting. If this is what Kierkegaard means by the absolute paradox, then it is a concept with little promise.

Fortunately, there is strong evidence that Kierkegaard does not mean a formal, logical contradiction when he terms the incarnation a 'contradiction'. First, we must recognise that the term 'contradiction' is not used solely or even mainly in this period to refer to a logical contradiction. The Hegelian philosophers who represent Kierkegaard's chief philosophical opposition use the term 'contradiction' to refer to any relation of opposition. For example, Hegel himself calls nature a contradiction, since nature is a union of contingency and necessity, irregularity and regularity, unpredictability and predictability.[13] It is clear that Hegel does not mean to claim that the existence of the natural world is a formal contradiction, but rather to call our attention to the incongruities and complexities that are found in our experience of nature.

Kierkegaard frequently uses the term 'contradiction' in just this way to refer to some relation of incongruity or experienced opposition. For example, he claims that all humour involves an awareness of 'contradiction'. We find it funny, he says, when a man looking up into the sky falls into a hole because of the contradiction between the upward gaze and the downward plunge.[14] Human existence itself is said to be contradictory, because it embodies a fundamental tension between the ideal requirements that we recognise as ethically binding and the human failings that characterise all of our lives.[15] This contradiction of existence is, as we shall see, particularly important to understand what is meant by the incarnation as a contradiction.

Most importantly, there are several passages in Kierkegaard's writings where a distinction is drawn between a contradiction in this broader sense of incongruity and a formal, logical contradiction. One of the clearest examples, though still not an easy passage to interpret, is from *Philosophical Fragments*.[16] In this work the pseudonym, Johannes Climacus, pretends to 'invent' the story of the incarnation, in which salvation, or 'knowing the Truth' is made possible for human beings by God himself having entered time to become the Teacher. The question concerns how people who live later than the time of the God's historical appearance can gain this truth. Can they receive it from one of the contemporary followers of the God, or must they get it directly from the God himself? Climacus argues that they must get it directly from the God, because if they get it from a contemporary follower we have a 'contradiction', which makes the supposition that the later generation could get the Truth from anyone else 'meaningless':

> That meaninglessness [the kind that comes from supposing a later follower could receive the Truth from someone other than the God], however, is unthinkable in a sense different from our stating that that fact [the Incarnation] and the single individual's relation to the god are unthinkable. Our hypothetical assumption of that fact and the single individual's relation to the god contains no self-contradiction, and thus thought can become preoccupied with it as with the strangest thing of all. That meaningless consequence, however, contains a self-contradiction; it is not satisfied with positing something unreasonable, which is our hypothetical assumption, but within this unreasonableness it produces a self-contradiction: that the god is the god for the contemporary, but the contemporary in turn is the god for a third party.[17]

The self-contradiction that is said to be meaningless here is clearly a formal, logical contradiction. The contemporary follower both is and is not the God. This person is not the God because the person himself received the Truth from the God. Yet this person is the God because he plays the role that only God can play by giving that same Truth to a later follower. The contradiction of the incarnation itself is not the same kind of contradiction; it may be 'the strangest of all things' but 'thought is free to occupy itself with it'. Thus it is clear that in this passage, and several others where a similar distinction is made, Kierkegaard denies that the incarnation is to be understood as a logical contradiction.[18]

It is clear that if Kierkegaard did think of the incarnation as a logical contradiction, it would completely fail to fulfil the functions he thinks the concept does fulfil. One important property of the absolute paradox for Kierkegaard is that it must be unique; the incarnation must somehow qualify as *the* absurd. However, there is nothing unique about a logical contradiction and no principled way to say that one is 'more contradictory' or 'absurd' than any other.

Furthermore, it is hard to see how a logical contradiction could serve as the 'boundary' or 'limit' of reason as the incarnation is supposed to do. To recognise a 'square circle' as a formal contradiction one must have a fairly clear grasp of the concepts of 'square' and 'circle'. In one sense at least, therefore, such a concept falls within the competence of reason; if it did not, reason could not properly classify it as a logical contradiction. The point of the incarnation, according to Kierkegaard, is that it is a concept that reason cannot understand. This is so not because reason has a perfectly clear grasp of what it means to be God and what it means to be human and properly judges that the two concepts are logically contradictory. In fact, just the reverse is the case. Human reason is baffled both by human nature and by God.[19] It is further baffled by the conjunction of the two concepts, but not because reason has a clear understanding of either what it means to be human or what it means to be God. The incarnation may *appear* or *seem* to human reason to be a logical contradiction, but it is not *known* to be such, and the believer does not think that it is a formal contradiction.

THE INCARNATION AND THE PARADOX OF EXISTENCE

But if the incarnation is not a formal contradiction, what kind of a contradiction is it? What is paradoxical about the 'absolute paradox'? To answer this question, we need to focus more closely on the elements of the contradiction. Kierkegaard consistently cites *temporality* and *eternity* as the contradictory or incongruous elements in the incarnation. How does he understand these concepts and what is contradictory about them?

If Kierkegaard were primarily a speculative philosopher, then I suppose it would make sense to interpret these concepts as logically contradictory, on the assumption that we can precisely describe the essence of each. However, Kierkegaard is not a speculative philosopher; his task is not disinterestedly to describe the essence of temporality and eternity as metaphysical concepts. Rather, for Kierkegaard, eternity and temporality are what we come to know in the process of existing as concrete human beings. Human existence itself is described by Kierkegaard as a 'contradiction' precisely because all human life is experienced as a constant attempt to synthesise time and eternity.[20]

The elements that compose the 'contradiction' of the incarnation are therefore precisely the elements that compose human existence generally. The idea that human existence is an on-going 'synthesis' of the temporal and the eternal is a pervasive one in Kierkegaard's writings, expressed most famously perhaps in one of the opening sentences of *The Sickness Unto Death*: 'A human being is a synthesis of the infinite and the finite, of the temporal and the eternal, of freedom and necessity'.[21] Human life is a continuous process of actualising conceptualised possibilities. What is conceived as a possibility is eternal and complete. Ideals as ideals are eternal: we seek the true, the good, the beautiful. However, when we attempt to realise these ideals in our own lives we always do so imperfectly, successively, incompletely. Such is the nature of temporal existence as we know it.

In one sense we know what it means to put temporality together with eternity, for that is what our own lives consist of. So the idea of the incarnation is not just a meaningless absurdity. Nevertheless, our experience of this 'synthesis' is that in time eternity is never fully realised. In fact, to say that the synthesis is never complete in this life is to say far too little, for such an assertion is compatible with the claim that the process of synthesis, while never finished, is still a continuous, harmonious approximation of a final realisation. In reality, however, all human beings experience life, at least at some points, as a process in which we diverge from our ideals. We do not merely fail to realise them completely, but find ourselves failing entirely.

As Kierkegaard sees it, Christianity is unique in holding that the eternal ideal that human life should seek to actualise exists – fully realised – in a temporal form. Such a realisation could not be straightforwardly perceived as an empirical fact. Nor do we find it natural to believe in such a possibility. The idea of the God-man strikes reason as 'the strangest of all things' because our universal experience is that the two are divergent. Our own temporality is at best a partial, incomplete realisation of the eternal, and it generally includes an experience of failure. Hence we find the idea that the eternal could be perfectly realised in a temporal existence baffling.

Our inability to comprehend this paradox is not therefore relative to the degree of intelligence that people have, since it is linked to a universal human characteristic, one that is present just as much in the genius as in the dull individual. Misunderstanding of the paradox

> consists in the delusion that the incomprehensibility of the paradox is supposed to be connected with the difference of greater and lesser understanding, with the comparison between good and poor minds. The paradox is connected essentially with being a human being, and qualitatively with each human being in particular, whether he has much or little understanding.[22]

The paradox is thus absolute in a way without being a logical contradiction. It may only be an apparent contradiction, but the appearance in this case is not grounded in differential human abilities.

The parallel between human existence generally and the incarnation does, however, help us to understand why Kierkegaard thinks this 'contradiction' has a unique importance and significance. In mirroring the structure of human existence, the incarnation has universal importance for humans because it reflects a universal dimension of human experience.

In speaking of the incarnation as a paradox that is above reason, I am giving a one-sided account of Kierkegaard's view. For he himself also speaks of this paradox as something that is *against* reason, and because of this he describes the incarnation not merely as the paradox, but as *the absurd*. I shall speak of this claim in the next chapter. However, I think it is important to recognise that there are two distinct claims being made, whether Kierkegaard himself recognised this or not. Even if one does not agree with Kierkegaard about the idea of the incarnation as being something that is absurd and against reason, one may still agree that the incarnation is something human reason cannot really understand.

Though he speaks a great deal about the theme of faith as the absurd which requires one to believe 'against the understanding', Kierkegaard at times does use the more traditional formula of faith as above the understanding, as in this passage from his *Journal*:

> Hugo de St. Victor states a correct thesis (Helfferich, *Mystik*, vol. I, p. 368): 'Faith is really not supported by the things which go beyond reason, by any reason, because reason does not comprehend what faith believes, but nevertheless there is something here by which reason becomes determined or is conditioned to honor the faith which it still does not perfectly succeed in grasping'.

> This is what I have developed (for example, in *Concluding Unscientific Postscript*) – that not every absurdity is the absurd or the paradox. The activity of reason is to distinguish the paradox negatively – but no more.[23]

Here faith is faith in the absurd, but 'the absurd' seems to be a particular kind of absurd, not to be confused with 'every absurdity'. This absurd or paradox is above reason and therefore not really supported by reason, but there is nonetheless some way in which reason can affirm what is above it. How this happens must still be explored, and I shall try to explain how faith is possible for Kierkegaard in the next chapter. However, before that, we will have to look at the full difficulty of believing by seeing why it is that Kierkegaard thinks that faith is against as well as above reason.

FAITH AND THE FINITUDE OF REASON

In exploring the theme of faith as above reason, we have continually hit upon the theme of the finitude of reason. For Aquinas, human reason is limited by the need of human thinking to ground itself in the senses; since God's essence cannot be sensed it therefore becomes necessary for God to reveal many truths about himself that must be accepted by faith. In a similar way, for Kant, the Idea of God transcends the limits of human reason, since reason can only achieve theoretical knowledge where it can employ concepts that relate to temporal experiences. Kant thinks this means that God can only be grasped through moral faith, when reason turns to its practical exercise and seeks the highest good as duty demands.

Kierkegaard shares the convictions of Aquinas and Kant about the finitude of human reason. In fact, the limitations imposed on reason by the historical, finite character of human reasoners is a major theme in his writings. Kierkegaard's philosophy contains a sustained polemic against Hegel and his followers, and the major point of contention is Kierkegaard's rejection of what he saw as the Hegelian claim that the individual thinker can rise to the level of 'pure thought'. Kierkegaard urges the thinker always to remember that he is a finite, existing human being, and to recognise fully the implications of this. The thinker who attempts to reach the standpoint of 'pure thought', or complete abstraction, is a comic figure, since such an undertaking still represents a choice on the part of a particular human being, and such a choice is always the expression of a passionate preference. 'Existing . . . cannot be done without passion'.[24] Yet the speculative thinker wants to see his systematic thought as the expression of a dispassionate understanding of the whole. The comic aspect lies in the fact that the speculative philosopher is absent-minded, for he has adopted an existential project that requires him to forget that he has any existential projects:

> It is from this side that an objection must first be made to modern speculative thought, that it has not a false presupposition but a comic presupposition, occasioned by its having forgotten in a kind of world-historical absent-mindedness what it means to be a human being . . .[25]

Kierkegaard clearly rejects any attempt on reason's part to produce 'the system', the final complete account of Reality as it is in itself, because to produce such a system, reason would have to assume 'the view from nowhere', the world seen from no particular place or perhaps from all angles simultaneously. When reason attempts to know the world, it can produce wonderful theories, but when those theories are applied to the actual world they can never be more than 'approximations', since both the world that is to be known and the knower are in constant temporal flux.[26] My knowledge of the world is both approximative and tentative, always subject to revision. As a temporal being I can never see the world as Spinoza attempted to do, 'under the aspect of eternity', as God himself sees things. 'Existence itself is a system – for God, but it cannot be a system for any existing human spirit'.[27]

The finitude that infects any attempt to develop a 'final system' of philosophy also shapes human knowledge in general. This uncertainty that characterises human knowledge of the eternal is doubly present when one encounters human history, since history is the realm of the contingent. History shares the contingency of all of the natural world; nothing that happens in time is necessary, since what is necessary, according to Kierkegaard, does not change.[28] The necessary is the timeless realm of logical necessity; it necessarily is what it is. The natural world is not that logical world, but the world of that which has 'come into existence'.[29] Hence this natural world is the world of change and therefore contingency, and this contingency is mirrored in the uncertainty of human knowing of that world. What is contingent could be or could have been otherwise, and so it cannot be a necessary truth that it has whatever characteristics it has.

However, besides the contingency of the natural world, human history involves the contingency of free human actions, actions that again could not be necessary without ceasing to be free. History involves a 'coming into existence within its own coming into existence'.[30] That is, human history shares not only the contingency of the natural world in general, but has a new level of contingency introduced by human free actions, which also involve a 'coming into existence'. It is easy to see, therefore, that the religious doctrine of the incarnation, in which God acts decisively within human history, cannot for Kierkegaard become the object of certain, objective knowledge. If the eternal has entered history, it cannot be the object of knowledge, at least not if knowledge is defined in an Enlightenment manner as a completely certain grasp of truth that rests purely on objective evidence.

However, the limits of the intellect in dealing with the incarnation do not stop with the general limits of historical knowledge. For the incarnation is described as the absolute paradox, the incomprehensible fact that reason cannot understand. So besides the uncertainty that is part of all historical knowledge, there is a special uncertainty that corresponds to the paradoxical nature of the object of belief. Corresponding to these two kinds of uncertainty are two different kinds of belief or faith, ordinary historical faith and faith 'in the eminent sense', that takes the incarnation as its object.[31]

FAITH, REVELATION AND AUTHORITY

It is not surprising, therefore, that for Kierkegaard religious truth lies above the capacities of finite, temporal human beings. God as eternal exceeds the power of human reason, and God as the eternal that has become temporal is doubly baffling. For Kierkegaard, this revelation on the part of God in human form should be believed because it has been authoritatively revealed. Any attempt to justify its content on philosophical grounds undermines the transcendent character of the revelation. It is a distinguishing mark of a genuine revelation that it 'did not arise in any human heart'; a revelation represents a break with all 'immanent' human thinking.[32]

The key element in a revelation is authority. Kierkegaard's thoughts on authority are spelled out in a book he wrote but did not publish. He called the work *The Book on Adler*, and it is translated into English as *On Authority and Revelation*. The book deals with a Danish priest, Adolph Adler, who claimed to have received a direct revelation from God, and was deposed by the Church on grounds of mental instability. (Kierkegaard probably did not publish the book out of consideration for Adler.) The case presented Kierkegaard with an ideal opportunity to reflect on how one might recognise a genuine revelation, and what accepting the authority of a revelation might mean. For Kierkegaard, a mark of a true prophet or apostle who has a genuine revelation is that the person demands faith on the basis of the authority of the revelation itself. If I claim to have a revelation, but then say you should believe it because I am a genius and can philosophically prove its content, I have undermined my own claim to have a revelation.[33]

If a child receives an order from a parent, but obeys the order only after establishing for herself that the behaviour commanded is good, then the child is not really accepting the authority of the parent.[34] Similarly, when one obeys a police order only when one has independently decided that the behaviour commanded is good, one does not really obey the order.[35] So, Kierkegaard argues, if we believe a revelation only when we have independently established the truth of the revelation, we do not really show we accept the authority of the revelation. We should not believe St Paul because St Paul is a genius, but accept what he says because Paul is an apostle:

> As a genius Paul can sustain no comparison with Plato or with Shakespeare, as an author of beautiful similes he ranks rather low, as stylist his is an obscure name, and as an upholsterer – well, I may admit that in this respect I don't know where to place him. One always does well to transform stupid seriousness into a jest – and then comes the really serious thing, the serious fact that Paul was an apostle, and as an apostle has no affinity either with Plato or Shakespeare or a stylist or an upholsterer, who are all of them (Plato as well as the upholsterer Hansen) beneath any comparison with him.[36]

Kierkegaard goes on to affirm that 'I am not obliged to obey Paul because he is clever or exceptionally clever, but I must submit to Paul because he has divine authority'.[37]

It is appropriate, Kierkegaard thinks, that God's decisive revelation is a paradox that human reason cannot confirm, for if we had the power to do so, we would thereby fail to show that we really trust God enough to obey and accept his authority.

Kierkegaard's basic argument that an authoritative revelation must be accepted on the basis of a trust in the authority of the revealer seems sound to me. If I only believe God when I have independently established the truth of what God tells me, then I do not really trust God. However, I do not think Kierkegaard fully recognises that rational inquiry about a revelation is not necessarily a sign of lack of faith in the revealer. A distinction should be made between critical questions about the content of what is revealed and critical questions about the credentials of the source.

It is true that I do not obey my parents if I only obey an order they have given me when I have independently decided that the action commanded would be a good one. However, suppose I receive an order that purports to be from my parents, but one that I have reason to doubt really comes from them? In that case, reflection on the order does not necessarily stem from lack of trust in the parents. If I look at the signature with care to see if it looks genuine, or reflect on whether or not this order is consistent with other orders I have received from them, then this may be because I desire to obey them, not because I am rebellious or insubordinate. Similarly, reflection on whether a revelation is really from God is not necessarily a symptom of a desire to evade God's authority.

Kierkegaard himself implicitly admits this in *On Authority and Revelation* when he tries to develop criteria to determine when a person is a genuine prophet or apostle. He argues, for example, that the true bearer of a revelation will trust in God's providence and not use worldly means to try to ensure the success of his cause.[38] But the application of such a criterion requires the use of reason. Hence, rational reflection on a revelation does not have to be an evasion of divine authority. It can be that, and will be that in the case where a person only is willing to accept the revelation when the content of that revelation has been independently verified as true. But critical reflection on whether a revelation is truly from God does not have to take this form.

Kierkegaard seems to consider the possibility of reflection on the credentials of the person claiming a revelation, but argues reason is of no help, because there can be no 'sensible certitude' that a person has a revelation. The genuine apostle 'has no other proof than his own assertion'.[39] Miracles or other accompanying characteristics are of no help, he thinks, because they require faith to be accepted. However, the fact that there can be no proof that a revelation is genuine does not imply that there cannot be criteria for a genuine revelation (some of which he suggests himself) such that there can be evidence for or against claims to revelation. The evidence may be such that it requires faith or spiritual sensitivity or some other quality rightly to discern and interpret it, but that does not mean that such evidence would necessarily be without value. A person who lacks proof that a revelation is genuine may still have good reasons for believing that it is; and relying on those reasons, provided they are reasons of the right kind, does not undermine the authority of the revelation.

THE PARADOX AND THE ABSURD

If Kierkegaard focused only on the incomprehensibility of God's revelation to human reason, his thought would not differ greatly from that of Thomas Aquinas. For, as we have seen, Aquinas also holds that God reveals truths to humans that must be believed because they are revealed. It is true that Kierkegaard, in stressing the paradoxicality of the revelation, makes its incomprehensibility more radical. It is not just that reason cannot determine the truth or falsity of the revelation, but reason finds the revelation utterly baffling. Another important difference is that Kierkegaard emphasises the character of the revelation as consisting of 'events'. It is in the actual events of the life of Jesus, understood as the Son of God, that God is revealed, and faith is belief in the reality of the God-in-time, rather than primarily being an acceptance of certain doctrines. These differences, however, may not be as great as they appear. Aquinas also stresses the mysteriousness of God's revelation, and he also understands that the doctrines are linked to historical events.

However, Kierkegaard does not merely argue that God's revelation in Jesus is a paradox that is incomprehensible to unaided human reason. One could say that he does not focus merely on human finitude and its inadequacy in understanding an infinite God. God is incomprehensible to finite humans. But Kierkegaard insists that this revelation is not merely incomprehensible, but also in some sense 'absurd' to natural human reason. Incomprehensibility is not itself to be equated with religious unbelief. Rather, unbelief has a deeper ground. For Kierkegaard, we shall see that faith turns out not to be merely above reason; it is also *against* reason. The ground for this is not merely finitude. It is human sinfulness. In the next chapter I shall explore this Kierkegaardian claim that faith is not only above but against reason by looking at the ways sin might impair the human ability to gain religious truth.

NOTES

1. For more about Kierkegaard's use of pseudonyms and his own relation to those characters see my *Kierkegaard's* Fragments *and* Postscript*: The Religious Philosophy of Johannes Climacus* (Atlantic Highlands, New Jersey: Humanities Press, 1983) Chps. 1 and 2. Also see my *Passionate Reason: Making Sense of Kierkegaard's* Philosophical Fragments (Bloomington, Indiana: Indiana University Press, 1992) Chp. 1.
2. See Immanuel Kant, *Critique of Pure Reason*, trans. Norman Kemp Smith (New York: St Martin's Press, 1965) p. 327.
3. Søren Kierkegaard, *Philosophical Fragments*, trans. Howard V. and Edna H. Hong (Princeton: Princeton University Press, 1985) p. 87.
4. For Kierkegaard's critique of proofs of God's existence, see *Philosophical Fragments*, pp. 39–44.
5. Søren Kierkegaard, *Concluding Unscientific Postscript*, trans. Howard V. and Edna H. Hong (Princeton: Princeton University Press, 1992) pp. 206–7n.
6. For an exploration of this and many other parallels between Kierkegaard and Kant, see Ronald M. Green, *Kierkegaard and Kant: The Hidden Debt* (Albany: SUNY Press, 1992).
7. See the discussion of Kant's account of the 'Antinomy of Reason' in Chp. 5 above, pp. 70–1.
8. *Philosophical Fragments*, pp. 36, 101. The former reference is an allusion to 1 Cor. 2:9.
9. Kierkegaard, *Philosophical Fragments*, p. 52 and many other places.
10. *Concluding Unscientific Postscript*, pp. 574–81.
11. *Concluding Unscientific Postscript*, p. 570.
12. For example, see Louis Pojman, *The Logic of Subjectivity* (University, Alabama: The University of Alabama Press, 1984) pp. 131–43.
13. See Hegel's *Philosophy of Nature*, trans. A. V. Miller (Oxford: Clarendon Press, 1979) pp. 17–22.
14. See the extended footnote in Kierkegaard, *Concluding Unscientific Postscript*, pp. 514n–19n. Kierkegaard assumes the man was not hurt in this case. Humour involves a 'painless' contradiction. A painful contradiction is tragic, rather than humorous.

15. The theme of existence as a 'contradiction' is pervasive in Kierkegaard's authorship. See, for example, *Concluding Unscientific Postscript*, pp. 82, 92.
16. *Philosophical Fragments*, pp. 100–2.
17. *Philosophical Fragments*, p. 101.
18. Besides the passage from *Philosophical Fragments* discussed above, there are at least two other passages that make this distinction. Perhaps the one that is most clear is from *Practice in Christianity*, trans. Howard V. and Edna H. Hong (Princeton, New Jersey: Princeton University Press, 1991) pp. 124–7. I believe that substantially the same point is made in *Concluding Unscientific Postscript*, p. 568, where a distinction is drawn between 'nonsense' and the 'paradox'. Also, see the claim in *Søren Kierkegaard's Journals and Papers*, trans. and ed. by Howard V. and Edna H. Hong (Bloomington, Indiana: Indiana University Press, 1967) p. 4, where it is said that 'not every absurdity is the absurd or the paradox. The activity of reason is in a negative manner to distinguish the paradox, but then no more.' For an extended discussion of all these passages see my *Kierkegaard's* Fragments *and* Postscript, pp. 212–19, and *Passionate Reason*, pp. 100–5.
19. See *Philosophical Fragments*, pp. 37–48.
20. *Concluding Unscientific Postscript*, p. 82.
21. Søren Kierkegaard, *The Sickness Unto Death*, trans. Howard V. and Edna H. Hong (Princeton: Princeton University Press, 1980) p. 13.
22. *Concluding Unscientific Postscript*, p. 566.
23. *Kierkegaard's Journals and Papers*, ed. and trans. by Howard V. Hong and Edna H. Hong (Bloomington, Indiana: Indiana University Press, 1967) Vol. I, p. 4 (entry #7).
24. *Concluding Unscientific Postscript*, p. 311.
25. *Concluding Unscientific Postscript*, p. 120.
26. *Concluding Unscientific Postscript*, p. 189.
27. *Concluding Unscientific Postscript*, p. 118.
28. *Philosophical Fragments*, pp. 76–8.
29. *Philosophical Fragments*, pp. 75–6.
30. *Philosophical Fragments*, p. 76.
31. Kierkegaard uses the Danish term *tro* which means both faith and belief. Ordinary historical faith or belief is distinguished from specifically Christian faith or belief in *Philosophical Fragments*, p. 87.
32. See Søren Kierkegaard, *On Authority and Revelation*, trans. Walter Lowrie (New York: Harper and Row, 1966) pp. 105f.
33. Kierkegaard thought that Adler had made just this mistake. After his initial claim to a revelation, Adler published four books in which he neither recants nor affirms his original claim to have had a revelation, but instead presents himself in the guise of a genius. For Kierkegaard this shows a fundamental confusion. See *On Authority and Revelation*, pp. 92–117, particularly pp. 101–8.
34. Kierkegaard himself uses this analogy in *On Authority and Revelation*, pp. 116–17.
35. *On Authority and Revelation*, pp. 110–11.
36. *On Authority and Revelation*, p. 105.
37. *On Authority and Revelation*, p. 107.
38. *On Authority and Revelation*, pp. 41–56.
39. *On Authority and Revelation*, pp. 117–18.

7

Faith Against Reason: Kierkegaard

Why does Kierkegaard so frequently assert that faith is not merely *above* but *against* reason? Faith is said to believe what is 'impossible' and 'absurd'.[1] Faith revels in the improbability of what is believed; a 'proof' of the content of what is to be believed, so far from being an aid to faith, would make faith impossible.[2] Can this be responsible fideism?

As we have noted, Kierkegaard is often understood to be asserting that faith involves a rejection of rationality altogether. If this were indeed Kierkegaard's view, I would urge that it be rejected, since I argued in Chapter 2 that such a rejection of reason cannot be rationally defended, and ultimately comes at a steep price for the fideist. Fortunately, I do not think that this irrationalism is a fair characterisation of Kierkegaard. As I also noted in Chapter 2, the term 'reason' is ambiguous. The concept is partly normative; it connotes those patterns of thinking that ought to be emulated because they are most likely to lead to truth. A purely normative concept is, however, abstract and empty. In reality every human society holds up particular concrete patterns and modes of thinking as constitutive of reason because they are thought to realise those normative ideals.

This descriptive content of reason is not beyond challenge, however. There is constant debate among philosophers concerning human perception, induction, testimony, self-evident principles, memory, and other cognitive practices. There are arguments about whether these practices need some kind of validation or backing to be rational, arguments about which are most 'basic' and reliable, arguments about the criteria within each practice for detecting reliable perceptions, memories, testimonies, etc.

So the question as to what practices actually constitute 'reason' is a real one that is the subject of ongoing debate.

Most sociologists argue, with a good degree of plausibility, that by and large what counts as 'reasonable' is what is accepted as reasonable in a society by those with the power and authority to shape the process of socialisation. We accept as reasonable what we are taught as reasonable, and those who control society also control what is transmitted through teaching.[3] The important French thinker Michel Foucault devoted almost his entire career to exploring the ways in which claims about reason, knowledge and truth reflect social power exerted by some over others.[4] Concrete judgments about what is rational are thus not dropped from Olympus, and it is thus quite conceivable that some individual might come to question whether the accepted judgments about what counts as 'reason' are those that in fact best realise the normative goals of reason. A critique of 'reason' is not *per se* a rejection of rationality, if rationality is a commitment to practices that are aimed at truth.

Suppose that a set of religious beliefs were true, but that the intellectual practices designated as 'reasonable' in a society (or in all human societies) were such as to make it impossible to recognise those truths. In that case, there would be a tension between the normative and descriptive aspects of reason. One might say that what is accepted as 'reason' concretely would be a barrier to achieving the goals of reason in an ideal normative sense. We might call these two different senses of reason the *concrete* and the *ideal* senses. I want to argue that a rejection of concrete reason is not necessarily a rejection of ideal reason, but may in fact be motivated by a commitment to ideal reason. My proposal is that some people who are called fideists, including Kierkegaard, are actually engaging in such a critique of concrete reason, though it is not always clear whether or not the fideists themselves clearly see the difference between the two forms of reason.

Of course such a proposal raises many questions. The person who rejects concrete reason must see it as suffering from some radical defects. If that were the case, one might wonder how human beings could ever come to recognise these defects. Must we not suppose that concrete reason is generally reliable if we are to detect particular instances where it is not reliable and in need of correction?

This is a pressing problem for critics of concrete reason and there are other problems as well. Nevertheless, I believe that this is precisely how Kierkegaard thinks about human reason and the truth of Christianity. He thinks that concrete human reason has a tendency to judge Christian faith irrational. Since the Enlightenment, though not only during that period, religious faith in general and Christian faith in particular have been under attack. Some theologians have thought it necessary to modify and reshape Christian faith so as to make it acceptable to reason, as Schleiermacher attempted to do when he defended religion against its 'cultured despisers'.[5] This strategy of reshaping religious beliefs to make them acceptable to modern culture is in fact the essence of what is often called 'modernism' or 'liberalism' in theology. For example, a common proposal has been to abandon any claims that miracles have occurred, or to abandon claims about the full deity of Jesus so as to make Christianity more acceptable to 'modern minds'.

Kierkegaard thinks that the appropriate Christian response to the intellectual attacks of modernity is to go on the offensive, rather than to attempt to shore up the battlements apologetically or to concede ground in the hope that some territory can still be preserved. The concrete human reason that wishes to indict faith is itself charged by him with being radically defective. Terminologically, he makes his point by conceding, or rather exuberantly asserting, that judged by the concrete standards of 'reason' faith is necessarily unreasonable. He then goes on to claim that the reason that makes this charge is itself 'a blockhead and a dunce'.[6]

One might wish that Kierkegaard had not been so quick to give the term 'reason' to the opponents of faith, by identifying 'reason' with what we have termed 'concrete reason'. His terminology here invites the misunderstanding that the person of faith simply does not care about truth, since reason in its normative sense is defined in terms of a search for truth. In attacking concrete reason under the label of 'reason', Kierkegaard might seem to be rejecting reason in the normative sense as well. However, Kierkegaard makes it clear that from his point of view, faith does aim at truth. In fact, he charges that a major reason people do not have faith is that they do not want truth; they prefer to believe what makes them happy. People prefer to live in illusions, even though the illusion masks the truth that their condition is one of despair, and they regard anyone who wishes to give them the truth about their condition as their enemy:

> It is far from being the case that men regard the relationship to truth, relating themselves to the truth, as the highest good, and it is very far from being the case that they Socratically regard being in error in this manner as the worst misfortune – the sensuous aspect in them usually far outweighs their intellectuality. For example, if a man is presumably happy, imagines himself to be happy, although considered in the light of truth he is unhappy, he is usually far from wanting to be wrenched out of his error . . . Why? Because he is completely dominated by the sensuous and the sensuous-psychical . . .[7]

Thus Kierkegaard reverses the common charge that religious belief is a form of wish-fulfilment, by claiming that this is true of religious *unbelief*. (However, he agrees with Freud that wish-fulfilment is characteristic of many inauthentic forms of religious faith as well.)

HOW SIN DAMAGES HUMAN REASON

We saw in the previous chapter that Kierkegaard agrees with Aquinas and Kant that faith is above human reason, because of the finitude and temporality of that human reason. The claim that faith is not only above but against human reason is rooted, not merely in the recognition of human finitude, but in the charge that human reason is radically defective. For Kierkegaard the damage is due to human sin.

How exactly is sin supposed to affect concrete human reason negatively? I believe that for Kierkegaard there are two primary ways that concrete reason is damaged by sin. I shall explain each in turn and then try to show that the two are in fact closely connected. Both kinds of damage presuppose that reason is a characteristic of actual persons, and that the reasoning of such persons is shaped by their character. The first kind of damage is that which is caused by reason's *pride* or what might be termed its imperialistic, domineering character. The second kind of problem is grounded in the *selfish* or egoistic character of reason. I shall first examine the damaging effects of pride.

Kierkegaard shares with Aquinas and Kant the conviction that God transcends the powers of the human mind, and he thinks that this limitation of human reason is particularly present when it comes to understanding God's incarnation in human form. By itself this seems to imply only that God as the object of faith is mysterious, something that is above reason. However, Kierkegaard combines this view of God as mysterious with some particular claims about the character of concrete human thinking.

Kierkegaard believes that reason has what we might term a restless, domineering quality, in that it is always striving to master or appropriate whatever it encounters. He claims that it is the supreme passion of all human thinking to 'want to discover something that thought itself cannot think'.[8] He claims that 'this passion is fundamentally present everywhere in thought'.[9] The attitude of reason is the attitude that wishes to explain, to make intelligible. When the scientist discovers some strange phenomenon, when something occurs that is unexpected and inexplicable in terms of current scientific theory, the scientist may indeed feel a sense of wonder and awe. That sense, however, is not the end but the beginning of scientific inquiry. The scientist is motivated to try to explain this new phenomenon, to make what is mysterious explicable. This recalcitrant reality must be mastered, forced to yield its secrets. When reason behaves in this way, Kierkegaard interprets it as seeking its own limits, testing each 'unknown' it encounters to see if it is truly resistant to reason's mastery.

Insofar as reason is confident that it will always be victorious in its continued quest, it will necessarily reject any claim that there is an *ultimate* mystery, anything that is in principle resistant to reason's domination and control. Kierkegaard thinks that this is precisely what might be termed the 'natural attitude' of human reason. Such an attitude of reason is really a claim of omniscience – not a claim of actual omniscience, but a claim that human reason as an infinite process of discovery is essentially omniscient. Two things become clear when reason is seen in this light.

1. We can easily see why faith is not merely above but is in some sense against reason. Faith is indeed above reason, but a reason that recognises its own limitations will not necessarily reject the possibility of faith. However, to the degree that reason insists that there is nothing that lies outside its power, it finds itself in tension with a faith that insists that its object exceeds reason's grasp.

2. We can also see why this natural tension between reason and faith is linked by Kierkegaard to sin. The classical Christian understanding of sin is to view sin as an expression of pride. Pride here is not the virtue of properly appreciating one's achievements; it is rather the vice of overestimating one's place in the universe. The Christian understanding of sin is that it involves a human being's confusion of himself or herself with God. In the Genesis account of the first temptation, the serpent offers the alluring line, 'You shall be as gods'. The sinful human being then sees himself or herself as the centre of the universe. The person sees himself or herself as completely self-sufficient, and therefore as possessing the final criterion of truth. The attitude is 'What (in principle) I cannot understand must be nonsense'. The understanding 'cannot get the paradox into its head', and thinks that this is an objection, even though in reality this claim is simply an echo of what the paradox says about itself and its relation to reason.[10] If there is a reality that is essentially mysterious to human reason, then such a prideful attitude is indeed damaging, because it blocks us from a recognition of this truth and from whatever kind of encounter and relation might be possible with such a mysterious reality.

The second feature of human sinfulness that Kierkegaard sees as damaging lies in what we could term the egoistic or selfish character of human reason. Of course human reason will not be flattered by this description of it as selfish, and it may well find it jarring. Reason in fact prides itself on its disinterestedness and objectivity.

Kierkegaard does not deny that a kind of disinterestedness on the part of reason is possible. Such objectivity, he says, is the glory of the scholar; it can be seen in the devoted historian, the scientist, the mathematician.[11] Strictly speaking, even this attitude is not purely disinterested; human reason cannot be absolutely pure, for human thinking is always the thinking of a concrete, existing human being. Even the objective scholar is motivated by interests of various kinds, and what Kierkegaard calls *pure thought* is a mirage that does not exist:

> Pure thinking is – what shall I say – piously or thoughtlessly unaware of the relation that abstraction still continually has to that from which it abstracts. Here in this pure thinking there is rest for every doubt; here is the eternal positive truth and whatever else one cares to say. This means that pure thinking is a phantom. And if Hegelian philosophy is free from all postulates, it has attained this with one insane postulate: the beginning of pure thinking.[12]

Abstract thought is possible. The objective scholar can have an interest in distancing himself from the subject, attempting to think about issues in ways that do not take into account his or her personal relation to the issues.

However, to the degree that this happens, the thinking of the scholar is divorced from existence. The scholar 'abstracts' from life, though he can never do so completely or purely. Insofar as a person is actually thinking about life and how life should be lived, such disinterestedness is not possible at all, according to Kierkegaard, because human actions and choices are moved by what he terms the passions. 'Existing, if this is not to be understood as just any sort of existing, cannot be done without passion'.[13] Merely thinking about a possibility is never sufficient to move an individual to act; one must care about the possibility, value it in some way. 'Am I the good because I think it, or am I good because I think the good? Not at all'.[14] Existential thinking, or thinking about life and what is related to life, is thus necessarily 'interested' thinking. 'For an existing person, existing is for him his highest interest, and his interestedness in existing is his actuality'.[15] Ethical and religious questions are pre-eminently questions about life and how it should be lived, and thus Kierkegaard argues that it is not possible to think in a purely neutral way about such questions.

Human beings think as whole persons. It is human beings who reflect, not brains or minds detached from concrete human persons. Their thinking therefore necessarily reflects the shape of their human interests and habits. One of the dominant characteristics of the thinking of sinful human beings is precisely its self-centred character. Even the disinterested scholar looks first to the index of a new book to see how many times he or she may be cited. A large proportion of human thinking is what might be termed 'cost-benefit analysis' – calculative thinking – and when we do our calculations, the cost and benefit to ourselves seems to weigh heavily, however much ethicists may prescribe a strict objectivity. Kant, whose ethic stressed the necessity of impartiality as much as anyone, nevertheless notes how pervasively we show our concern for what he terms 'the dear self'.[16]

For Kierkegaard human understanding is 'the stockbroker of the finite', that power we have to calculate the relative value of goods and the costs associated with them.[17] What we might call the self-interested character of human reasoning for Kierkegaard comes through clearly in a satirical passage in which he pokes fun at the 'sensible individual' who allows faith to be supported by (and controlled by) rational arguments:

> See, the wader feels his way with his foot, lest he go out so far that he cannot touch bottom. In the same way, with his understanding, the sensible person feels his way in probability and finds God where probability suffices, and thanks him on the great festival days of probability when he has obtained a really good job and there is the probability of quick advancement to boot. And he thanks him when for a wife he finds a girl both beautiful and congenial, and even Councillor of War Marcussen says that it will be a happy marriage, that the girl has the kind of beauty that in all probability will last a good time, and that she is built in such a way that in all probability she will bear healthy and strong children. To believe against the understanding is something else, and to believe with the understanding cannot be done at all, because the person who believes with the understanding talks only about job and wife and field and oxen and the like, which are in no way the object of faith.[18]

Kierkegaard here seems to be saying that human thinking not only deals with what is finite, but considers that finitude in a self-interested way.

The implication of this is that the story of the incarnation is doubly impervious to human reason. For the story of the God-man is not merely the story of what is infinite. It is a story of love – pure self-giving love. The God who gives himself for humans is a God who does not need human beings at all. His motivation for becoming human to redeem us can only be a love that differs from every human love.[19] For all human love, even the purest love of parent for child, or the grandest romantic passion, aims at least partly at self-satisfaction. We love, but our love does not aim simply at the benefit of the other, but also at our own happiness. The kind of love that God's incarnation represents is therefore a love of which we have no experience at all apart from the incarnation itself.

Kierkegaard accepts the ancient maxim that 'like can only be known by like'. Because we ourselves have never loved in the manner that God loves, it is a love we cannot understand. The person who is selfish naturally sees the actions of others as motivated by the same desires. Our natural response is suspicion; there must be an angle, we think. 'What's in it for God, anyway?' we cynically wonder. We find ourselves sceptical even when confronted with apparently altruistic human behaviour, but the reckless lack of concern for his own privilege that God displays in becoming human totally goes beyond our understanding:

> Divine compassion, however, the unlimited *recklessness* in concerning oneself only with the suffering, not in the least with oneself, and of unconditionally recklessly concerning oneself with *each* sufferer – people can interpret this only as a kind of madness over which we are not sure whether we should laugh or cry.[20]

Because of our sinful self-centredness, we cannot do anything but find this story the 'strangest possible thing',[21] the 'most improbable thing' we can imagine.[22]

The incarnation cannot be understood because it is a story of how the absolutely different (God), moved by unfathomable love, has become absolutely human. But what is the difference between the divine and the human that makes such an understanding so difficult? Kierkegaard says unequivocally that the difference lies in human sinfulness.[23] The problem is not fundamentally the speculative problem of seeing how a being with properties like omnipotence and omniscience could become human, even though Kierkegaard has no doubt that this theoretical task is one that human reason cannot accomplish. That theoretical failure, however, only means that faith is above reason. It is sin that makes faith appear to be against reason. The problem is that God's nature is love and we are so self-centred that we cannot understand God's love, even when, especially when, it is expressed in human form.

There is of course a link between the two ways sin operates to damage our rational capacities. It is our self-centredness that makes us prideful and self-sufficient. It is because we are so fundamentally concerned with self that we want to make ourselves the centre of the universe and become as gods. Or, looking at things from the other direction, it is our prideful self-sufficiency that makes it impossible for us to love, that blocks us from truly seeing and caring about the other for the other's sake.

CAN REASON RECOGNISE ITS OWN LIMITS?

In the series of movies that made him famous, Clint Eastwood played a character who often informed a villain (before dispatching him to the next life) 'A man's gotta know his limitations'. Indeed, it is beneficial for all of us to know our limits. However, if human reason is as limited as Kierkegaard maintains, can this be recognised? If reason is so damaged, then it appears that it will be unable to recognise that it has been damaged.

Kierkegaard maintains that one of the effects of sin is typically to blind reason to the damaging effects of sin. Self-deception or what Marxists call 'false consciousness' is indeed the common condition of human thinking. However, Kierkegaard does not think that a recognition of the limits of reason is impossible for reason. It is true that he says that the 'natural' response of reason to the God-man as the object of faith is to be offended. However, it is very important to see that this 'natural' response is not inevitable; it is not the only possible response. Nor is it in any objective sense more 'rational' than the other option, which is to respond in faith.

The two possible relations between reason and the incarnation, that paradox which is the object of faith, are illustrated by Kierkegaard through an analogy with romantic love. It is true, he says, that reason has 'strong objections' to the paradox, since 'the understanding certainly cannot think it, cannot hit upon it on its own, and if it is proclaimed, the understanding cannot understand it'.[24] Yet, there is also something about the paradox that attracts reason, since reason is steadily seeking 'that which thought cannot think'. Reason is in fact trying to discover its own ultimate limit, 'seeking its own downfall'.[25] To see the two possible relations between reason and the paradox, we must look at romantic love:

> Self-love lies at the basis of love, but at its peak its paradoxical passion wills its own downfall. Erotic love also wills this, and therefore these two forces are in mutual understanding in the moment of passion, and this passion is precisely love . . . So also with the paradox's relation to the understanding, except that this passion has another name, or rather, we must simply try to find a name for it.[26]

The name he ultimately decides to give this passion is, unsurprisingly, faith.

I believe that the thought that underlies this somewhat obscure passage is something like this. Self-love and genuine love appear to be at odds; it looks as if egoism and altruism are opposing orientations. However, romantic love, when it becomes genuine love, overcomes this opposition. It is true that love begins as self-love; the lover initially wants to be with the loved one out of a desire for the lover's own happiness. However, as love grows, and the lover really begins to care for the other person, happiness comes from seeking the happiness of that other. In this relation self-love 'founders but is not annihilated'.[27] Self-love fulfils its goal of personal happiness by in a sense relinquishing it, ceasing to make egoistic satisfaction its primary end.

Of course not everyone is capable of such love, and Kierkegaard says that the person who, out of selfishness, shrinks from love, cannot really understand love and is incapable of grasping it.[28] The idea seems to be that one's ability to conceive of love depends on whether one has been gripped by the passion itself. The selfish person becomes embittered by love, perhaps sensing unconsciously that in rejecting love, the person is in fact rejecting what he or she truly wants.

Returning to the relation between reason and the paradox, faith and offence are clearly supposed to be analogous to love and the embittered selfishness that shrinks from love. If offence is more 'natural' than faith, the ground for this clearly lies in the character of human nature as it concretely is. When reason is willing to recognise its own limits, as Kant and Aquinas urge it to do, then Kierkegaard says it can find fulfilment. When reason shrinks from such a recognition, obstinately and imperialistically insisting on its own completeness and autonomy, then it becomes bitter and angry at what it refuses, much as the selfish egoist becomes bitter and angry at love. The crucial point is that faith and offence are opposite *passions*. It is not cool rationality that determines the response of reason to the object of faith, but the nature of the passion that grips the reasoner.

Kierkegaard's claim then is that human reason is not inevitably offended by the Christian revelation, even if offence is in some sense 'natural'. Reason can itself recognise its limits. As Kierkegaard puts it, faith is the happy passion in which 'reason limits itself, the paradox bestows itself'.[29] The prevalence of offence and the widespread tension between reason and the paradox, a tension that makes it necessary for faith to be defined as something that goes against reason, are both due to the imperialistic and egoistic character of human reasoners. To come to faith reason must recognise both its finitude and its own 'damaged' character; it must see that its tendency to reject the object of faith is due to a prideful, egoistic character that is in fact an impediment to truth. To acquire the ability to believe the paradox and avoid offence, people must acquire a new passion that will reshape their characters from the ground up.

HOW CAN A DAMAGED REASON RECOGNISE ITS PROBLEMS?

A serious problem emerges at this point for any view of faith and reason that is like Kierkegaard's. Perhaps it is possible that reason is indeed defective in the ways Kierkegaard alleges. However, if this is so, then it may appear that reason will be powerless to discover this truth, for if reason is fundamentally damaged, then it would seem impossible for it to recognise the damage. It is precisely this point that underlies the criticisms made in Chapter 2 against fideists such as Van Til, who appear to endorse such a view of the total helplessness of reason. Is Kierkegaard subject to the same type of criticism?

Kierkegaard himself considers the competency of reason by looking at the figure of Socrates, considered as a paradigm of rational thought. For Kierkegaard, the ability of human reason to discover Truth is symbolised in the Platonic doctrine of recollection, here attributed to Socrates.[30] Recollection affirms that Truth is within human beings; at least the essential capacity to grasp Truth is, and it is the capacity or ability that is crucial.[31] If Recollection were valid, then humans would be autonomous and would have no need of any special revelation from God. From this Socratic viewpoint, a human being can teach another human being, but when such teaching occurs, the teacher should understand his or her essential equality with the learner. Socrates understood this, and saw himself simply as a 'midwife' who helped others to grasp the Truth that was present within them already.[32] The Socratic teacher sees himself only as an 'occasion' for the other to acquire what belongs to humans as humans. 'Viewed Socratically, any point of departure in time is *eo ipso* something accidental, a vanishing point, an occasion. Nor is the teacher anything more . . .'[33]

When put into this language, the Christian critique of 'reason' is a claim that Recollection is not possible for humans; we have within us neither the Truth nor the capacity to discover the Truth.[34] Instead we need a Teacher who can bring us the Truth, and even more important, transform us into the kind of beings who can grasp the Truth. For Kierkegaard this means the Teacher must be God himself, for only God can transform a person in such a fundamental way that the person is essentially re-created. Thus the Christian narrative of the incarnation requires a rejection of the assumption of Recollection.

However, within the Christian picture, is there any room for anything resembling Recollection, any remnant of autonomy? For Kierkegaard there is one point of analogy between the Socratic picture of Truth and the Christian picture. The Christian view is that human beings do not possess the Truth but are in fact in a state of Untruth.[35] The first thing the God who is to be my teacher must impart to me is the truth about my condition of being in Untruth. It is only if I learn that I am in Untruth that Christianity begins to makes sense to me. But if the learner can make this discovery, then there is a possibility that he or she will gain a kind of understanding of Christianity, or at least an understanding of why Christianity cannot be understood by autonomous reason. With regard to the discovery of my Untruth, Kierkegaard says that 'the Socratic principle applies: the teacher is only an occasion, whoever he may be, even if he is a god, because I can only discover my own untruth by myself, because only when *I* discover it is it discovered, not before, even though the whole world knew it'.[36] Within the Christian account of things, 'this becomes the one and only analogy to the Socratic'.[37]

On this crucial question, then, Kierkegaard recognises that even a 'damaged' reason must not be so damaged that it is impossible for it to recognise the truth about its condition. Does this mean that the defective character of reason is not taken seriously or that reason is not really so damaged as initially appears? I do not think that it does. Even to recognise its sinful 'untruthful' character reason may need assistance. The Kierkegaardian account does not imply that reason can discover its problematic character all by itself; if that were the case, then it would seem that reason would be in pretty good shape after all. The discovery of my Untruth is precipitated by a revelation in which I meet God and in light of that meeting come to understand myself in a new way. So Kierkegaard has not really reverted to a faith in the soundness of autonomous reason.

Nevertheless, if we take seriously the historical character of reason, reason should be open to the possibility of such a 'transformative encounter'. If reason is a capacity that is developed in time, both individually and socially, then we must recognise that people do at times acquire insights that what they previously took to be 'rational' is not in fact 'truth-conducive'. The child learns that a particular pattern of reasoning is in fact fallacious. The scientist discovers that apparently 'self-evident' assumptions about the character of space and time are not really self-evident after all. How are such discoveries made? Typically, they are made when the ideas of the person we might call 'the learner' are challenged by someone else who thinks differently. Such changes require an encounter with an 'Other', an encounter in which the learner is changed.

The contemporary Jewish philosopher Emmanuel Levinas has much to say about the encounter with 'the Other'.[38] Levinas has argued that much of modern Western philosophy has been turned inward into self-consciousness. The focus has been on epistemology, with the search for truth rooted in the certainty of self-consciousness. Levinas argues for 'ethics' instead of epistemology as 'first philosophy', but by 'ethics' he does not mean simply systematic thinking about ethical theories, but a kind of philosophical thinking that takes as its starting point 'the gaze of the Other'. It is when I look into the face of the Other that I come to understand my own character.

Kierkegaard would I think be sympathetic to Levinas's claim that to know the truth people must not simply burrow into their own consciousness, but open themselves up to the transforming look of the Other. His worry, however, concerns our ability to see the Other in the right way. All around the world the sorry tale of ethnic strife and racism shows that the persistent human response to the Other is to fail to see the Other as my neighbour. Kierkegaard thinks that in order properly to see the Other who is my human neighbour as a neighbour, I must first allow myself to be transformed by the gaze of the Other who allowed himself to be crucified for my sake.

It does seem possible therefore for Kierkegaard to hold both that reason suffers from some major defects, but also that reason might be able to recognise those defects under certain conditions. The conditions in question include some kind of transformative encounter which enables reason to understand something about its condition.

Of course it by no means follows that because reason can recognise its condition that it has the ability to change that condition.[39] Just as I might, for example, recognise that my eyesight is bad without being able to remedy the problem, so also I might come to see that my 'natural' reasoning is corrupted by pride and egoism without being able to transform myself so as to become humble and loving. The recognition of the problem, while it may be a precondition to a solution, is not the solution itself.

We could imagine such a transformative encounter as simply producing a new perspective in the learner automatically; in such a case we might say the learner has simply been 'overpowered' by the experience. This would be analogous to the assertion by Van Til that the only remedy for human sinfulness is for God to 'force an entry'. However, Kierkegaard does not envision the encounter along these lines, because God chose to reveal himself in the form of a humble human being. God could of course have used his omnipotence to ensure that the learner is transformed, but by doing so the learner would have been 'crushed'.[40] God's love is such that he desires the learner to respond to him freely and out of love. In revealing himself in the paradoxical form of the humble servant, God makes it possible for the learner to come to see God's true character (pure love), and, in contrast, the learner's own selfishness. However, God also makes it possible for the learner to refuse the insight offered. After all, the one who claims to be divine cannot be immediately recognised as God, since to all outward appearances he is an ordinary human being.

In the final analysis, therefore, Kierkegaard offers us a form of responsible fideism which is not like the irrational fideisms criticised in Chapter 2. It is true that Kierkegaard argues that the Christian view of faith is that it requires autonomous reason to 'surrender' or 'yield itself' to God's revelation.[41] However, he also insists that it is possible for reason itself to recognise the need for this. In one sense the autonomy of reason is respected; reason is not set aside in an authoritarian manner, but *sets itself aside*.[42] When the individual is gripped by the passion of faith, then reason and God's paradoxical revelation 'are on good terms'.[43] Since the encounter with God does not force the new insight on reason, it is also possible for reason to recoil from the revelation, in that passionate clinging to autonomy that Kierkegaard calls offence. However, Kierkegaard stresses that though offence is in one sense natural (and thus faith must be understood as 'against' reason as it functions apart from the transforming encounter), offended reason is no more 'rational' than reason that has been transformed by faith. Faith and offence are 'opposite passions'. Both stem from the passionate response of the person who has encountered God's revelation in Jesus.

DOES KIERKEGAARD LEAVE ROOM FOR OBJECTIVE REASONING?

My discussion has focused on what seems to me to be the central and deepest element in Kierkegaard's critique of reason. However, there are many other fideistic elements in his thought. His arguments often contain valuable insights, but in some cases these insights are mingled with claims that I do not think are defensible.

Perhaps the strongest critique of Kierkegaard's fideistic arguments is found in Robert Adams' article, 'Kierkegaard's Arguments Against Objective Reasoning in Religion'. Adams discusses and criticises three arguments he finds in Kierkegaard against objective reasoning in religion: the approximation argument, the postponement argument and the passion argument. Adams finds the first argument to be mistaken; the other two have some plausibility but depend on a conception of religious faith that he does not wish to accept. In all three cases Adams rightly focuses on Kierkegaard's view that Christian faith contains historical beliefs, and thus raises the question of the relation of such faith to historical inquiry and evidence.

The approximation argument hinges on the claim that historical evidence, on Kierkegaard's view, can never be completely certain, but can only lead to a belief that has a certain level of probability. However, as Adams reads Kierkegaard, religious faith involves an 'infinite interest' in the truth of at least some of its beliefs, and there is an incommensurability between such an infinite interest and even the smallest chance of error.[45] Or, as Kierkegaard says, 'in relation to an eternal happiness, and an impassioned, infinite interest in this (the former can be only in the latter), an iota is of importance, of infinite importance . . .'[46]

Adams rightly points out that this argument does not really show that reasoning is not of value to the religious believer. It does show, he thinks, that for a person with such an 'infinite interest' in the truth of a belief, even the smallest possibility of error would be of concern.[47] However, Adams argues that the believer may still *reason* that he or she is justified in disregarding the chance of error, because the chances of not satisfying the infinite interest will be much greater if this is not done. For example, suppose that I have a passionate desire for eternal life, and believe that there is a 99 per cent probability that I will receive it if I believe in the truth of a particular doctrine. It is true that I may rightly worry about the chance of error, since the stakes are so high, but it is also true that my chance of achieving my goal will be much greater if I follow the probabilities here and ignore the uncertainty. In some sense this is the rational thing for me to do.

I think Adams is quite right about this, but I am not sure that the point is really a criticism of Kierkegaard. When Kierkegaard argues that faith should not be based on objective reasoning he has in mind what I would term evidential scholarship, inquiry that focuses solely on the objective probability of the truth of the belief, with no consideration given to the subjective desires of the individual. Kierkegaard does not wish to reject thinking or reflection altogether. In fact, a substantial portion of *Concluding Unscientific Postscript* is an exploration of what he calls 'subjective thinking', which is thinking that is, we might say, situated by taking account of the needs and desires of the thinker.[48] The argument that Adams presents, however, is manifestly one that does take into account the situation of the potential believer. It does not focus solely on the probability of the belief but rather says that belief makes sense because it is the best way for the believer to realise his or her desires.

So it seems correct that Adams has demonstrated that Kierkegaard's argument does not show that what Adams calls 'objective thinking' is not valuable for faith, but it is not clear that Kierkegaard means to reject this kind of thinking. I think that Adams has in fact missed the heart of

Kierkegaard's concern, which does not lie in the approximative character of historical evidence, but in the incommensurability between such evidence and the passionate commitment which faith demands.

Something like this problem of incommensurability underlies the second argument Adams finds in Kierkegaard, what Adams calls the 'postponement argument'. The idea here is that historical inquiry is never completed, and thus historical beliefs based on such inquiry must always be tentative. It is always possible, at least theoretically, that new evidence will emerge that will overturn any historical conviction. Thus, if religious beliefs were based on such evidence, they would have to be of this tentative character. Kierkegaard thinks, however, that religious beliefs should have a kind of finality that differs from this kind of scholarly judgment. Even if Kierkegaard is wrong to say that such evidence has no bearing on religious belief, it seems right to claim that religious beliefs with the right kind of decisiveness will not stem solely from such 'objective' evidential concerns, but will be motivated by subjective needs and desires.

In fact, Kierkegaard's concern here is very similar to that of William James, in the argument for 'the will to believe' that was discussed in Chapter 3.[49] I interpreted James's argument there as a form of anti-evidentialism. Specifically, following George Mavrodes, I argued that James wishes to reject what could be called proportionality evidentialism, which holds that belief must be proportioned to evidence. Even if belief requires some evidence (a threshold requirement), it does not follow that the character of a belief is determined solely by evidence. What Mavrodes calls the 'meatloaf factor', an asymmetry between the value of the consequences of believing and disbelieving, helps determine the amount of evidence we require and also may give the belief a qualitative character that does not come only from evidence.

Kierkegaard's argument can also be understood as a rejection of evidentialism; perhaps he can be understood as rejecting both proportionality and threshold evidentialism. Like James (and Pascal) he wants to argue that if you want something like an eternal happiness more than anything else, then it may be reasonable to commit yourself wholeheartedly to something that promises to help you obtain it, even if the chances of obtaining what you seek are not high because the objective probability that eternal happiness is truly to be gained in this way is not high either. Perhaps Kierkegaard wishes to argue that if your desire for this good is great enough (infinitely high, whatever that might mean), then even a very low probability would be sufficient to motivate belief, so that a passionate believer simply ceases to worry about evidence at all. We might say that for such a believer any amount of evidence at all will be sufficient.

Of course one way that this might occur will be if the beliefs in question are *basic* in character, as Plantinga has argued.[50] If a belief is not based on evidence at all, then it will not be affected by the quality or quantity of the evidence, and the kind of incommensurability that Kierkegaard sees between scholarly inquiry and religious faith will not be a problem. Of course even basic beliefs for Plantinga require a ground of some kind, a situation in which a true belief is elicited through some process or mechanism that is designed to produce such a belief. One way to think about Kierkegaard's claims about subjectivity is to see them as claims about the character of the ground of religious beliefs.[51] The specifically Christian beliefs he is discussing, for example, can be understood as beliefs that require a particular set of emotions (or 'passions' in Kierkegaard's language). A person cannot come to believe in Christ without a strong sense of sinfulness and a desperate desire for God's forgiveness. Those are the factors that produce the beliefs. When they are present, the evidence is always sufficient; when they are lacking, no amount of evidence is enough.[52]

This interpretation of Kierkegaard as arguing that religious beliefs should be understood as basic in character, and grounded partly in subjective factors, also helps us understand the third argument that Adams attributes to Kierkegaard. The final argument that Adams considers is what he terms the 'passion argument'. The claim here is not that there is never enough objective evidence to produce the certainty that faith demands. Rather, the claim is that faith does not even want objective certainty; it thrives on uncertainty:

> The almost probable, the probable, the to-a-high-degree and exceedingly probable – that he can almost know, or as good as know, to a higher degree and exceedingly almost *know* – but *believe* it, that cannot be done, for the absurd is precisely the object of faith and only that can be believed.[53]

The true religious believer is like a lover who does not need probable arguments that the beloved is worth loving. A need for such an argument would be a sign that love is in fact fading. The genuine lover actually welcomes a chance to show the genuineness of the love by running risks and paying a price:

> it never occurs to a girl truly in love that she has purchased her happiness at too high a price, but rather that she has not purchased it at a price high enough . . . so it is also the case with the highest that you get what you pay for.[54]

Adams objects that this passion argument does not take into account the dispositional character of faith. It may be true that faith requires a willingness to undergo risks if necessary, but a willingness to run such risks does not mean that one must actually run them. There is a parallel here with the love relationship; perhaps a genuine lover shows love by continuing to love even when there is reason to doubt. However, a willingness to do that does not mean love requires the doubt to be actual.

I think that Adams is correct to argue that even if faith involves a willingness to believe in the face of difficulties, this does not mean that one must actually have the difficulties in order to have genuine faith. I have faith in my wife if I am willing to believe in her even when I have evidence that she has wronged me; however, I do not have to be in the situation where it appears she has wronged me to have this faith in her.

However, it is true that love may grow and develop in ways that it would not otherwise when it is tested. And it may also be the case that faith may similarly grow and develop in ways that it would not otherwise when it is tested by uncertainty. So even if faith does not require uncertainty, it may welcome it, and perhaps this is all Kierkegaard really needs to maintain. For it appears that our world offers opportunities enough for uncertainty, both for those who possess religious faith and those who are committed to some secular faith.

DEFEATERS AND THE VALUE OF EVIDENCE

In the end, however, I believe that Kierkegaard does go too far in dismissing the value of evidence. He may be right in claiming that faith is properly basic and not based on evidence. He may also be right in claiming that faith has qualities that stem from its grounds in what he terms 'subjectivity'. Objective evidence may be neither necessary nor sufficient for faith. However, it does not follow from this that objective evidence is simply irrelevant for faith, or that the believer will have no concern for evidence.

Even a belief that is properly basic is subject to being 'defeated' or overturned by evidence. As Plantinga develops the notion, properly basic beliefs are not infallible, and Kierkegaard, with his stress on human finitude and sinfulness, would certainly agree that a human being must admit to the possibility of being mistaken. So I believe, right now, in a basic manner, that I had pancakes for breakfast this morning. However, if I return to the house and discover that I left bowls of half-eaten cereal in the kitchen sink, and see no evidence of pancake preparation, I am prepared to admit that my belief is false. So a claim that a belief is basic does not imply that it is immune to falsification.

Of course if the original ground for my belief is strong enough, I may simply cling to the belief and reject the defeater. Perhaps someone sneaked into my house, cleaned up the pancake makings, and then left the appearances of a cereal breakfast in order to deceive me. It is not always clear when it is reasonable to think a belief has been defeated, and when to continue to hold it in the face of new evidence that cuts against it.

In the case of a religious belief that has historical content, such as Kierkegaard thinks is the case for Christianity, it seems wrong to say that the believer would always be right to ignore evidence that falsified the belief. Suppose, for example, that we found overwhelmingly powerful evidence that Jesus never existed, and that the whole of Christianity, along with its early history, had been invented in the fifth century. If the evidence were really powerful, would it still be possible to continue to believe that an historical figure from first-century Palestine, Jesus of Nazareth, was divine?[55]

So even if religious beliefs are basic in character, I doubt that evidence can be simply ignored or dismissed as irrelevant. However, the heart of Kierkegaard's position can I think still be maintained. What he wants to assert is that faith, with all its passion and decisiveness, does not stem from evidence. That may be true, even if it is important to the believer that there is no decisive evidence that would disprove his or her belief. The intellectual inquiry and amount of evidence that might be necessary in order to 'defeat the defeater' is quite different than what would be required if the belief itself were based simply in objective evidence. It may be important for the believer that there is no overwhelmingly powerful evidence that the story of Jesus was invented in the fifth century; it may not be important that the historical truth of the story cannot be proved to secular historians.[56]

As we shall see in the next chapter, when I examine the project of looking for evidence for God's existence, it is not always clear that evidence precludes the need for faith, or that faith considers evidence unimportant. There may be evidence that can only be seen as evidence by the eyes of faith, but such evidence might still be important for those who have those eyes of faith. Perhaps Kierkegaard draws too sharp a distinction between 'objective' and 'subjective' ways of thinking about religious truths. Pure objectivity may be a myth, as he himself argues. But pure subjectivity may be mythical as well, particularly if religious questions are ones that have real answers, answers that may be true or false. For one of our deepest subjective concerns is truth.

But this objection to Kierkegaard, even if it is sound, does not touch what I take to be his deepest concerns, which are I think twofold: an emphasis on the ways that sinfulness and finitude limit human thinking, and on the ways that certain emotions and passions are necessary in order to get at religious truth. If Kierkegaard is right, then a good deal of the intellectual practices and attitudes that are taken as 'reasonable' by sinful human beings do not in fact help us get on track with truth. To make contact with truth we need to be reshaped from the ground up, and for Kierkegaard that requires a reorientation of our deepest desires.

NOTES

1. Actually, these terms are usually found in Kierkegaard's pseudonymous writings and there is some debate about whether or not this language is characteristic of Kierkegaard's own position. See Chapter 6, n. 1 for more about the problem of pseudonymity.
2. Søren Kierkegaard, *Concluding Unscientific Postscript*, trans. by Howard V. and Edna H. Hong (Princeton: Princeton University Press, 1992) pp. 211, 233.
3. A very strong version of this claim is found in the so-called 'strong program' in the sociology of knowledge, which tries to explain all beliefs as accepted for social reasons, reasons that cannot be linked to objective truth or transcendent rationality. For an example, see Barry Barnes and David Bloor, 'Relativism, Rationalism, and the Sociology of Knowledge', in *Rationality and Relativism*, ed. Martin Hollis and Steven Lukes (Cambridge, Massachusetts: MIT Press, 1984) pp. 21–47. One does not have to accept this strong claim and its accompanying relativism to accept the weaker thesis that a great deal of what is accepted as 'reason' is due to sociological factors.
4. For a good brief account of Foucault's thinking, see his 'Afterword' that appears at the end of Hubert L. Dreyfus and Paul Rabinow, *Michel Foucault: Beyond Structuralism and Hermeneutics* (Chicago: University of Chicago Press, 1983). For longer statements of Foucault's views, see Gordon Colin, ed., *Power/Knowledge: Selected Interviews and Other Writings, 1971–77* (New York: Pantheon, 1980) and Paul Rabinow, ed., *The Foucault Reader* (New York: Pantheon, 1985).
5. See Friedrich Schleiermacher, *On Religion: Speeches to its Cultured Despisers*, trans. John Oman (New York: Harper, 1958).
6. Søren Kierkegaard, *Philosophical Fragments*, trans. Howard V. and Edna H. Hong (Princeton: Princeton University Press, 1985) p. 53 (translation modified).
7. Søren Kierkegaard, *The Sickness Unto Death*, trans. by Howard V. and Edna H. Hong (Princeton: Princeton University Press, 1980) pp. 42–3 (translation modified).
8. *Philosophical Fragments*, p. 37.
9. Ibid.
10. *Philosophical Fragments*, p. 53.
11. See, for example, Kierkegaard's praise of the critical Biblical scholar who tries to establish the Biblical text accurately and understand its origin historically. He says that this kind of scholarship deserves our admiration except, as is so often the case, when it implies that this scholarly work has some implications for faith. See *Concluding Unscientific Postscript*, pp. 24–6. In another passage (*Postscript*, p. 193) he says the indifference of the scholar is the basis of the objective validity of the work of the mathematician or historian.
12. *Concluding Unscientific Postscript*, p. 314.
13. *Concluding Unscientific Postscript*, p. 311.
14. *Concluding Unscientific Postscript*, p. 330.
15. *Concluding Unscientific Postscript*, p. 314.
16. Immanuel Kant, *Grounding for the Metaphysics of Morals*, 3rd edn trans. James W. Ellington (Indianapolis, Indiana: Hackett Publishing Co., 1993) p. 20.
17. Søren Kierkegaard, *Fear and Trembling*, trans. Howard V. and Edna H. Hong (Princeton: Princeton University Press, 1983) p. 36.
18. *Concluding Unscientific Postscript*, p. 233.
19. See *Philosophical Fragments*, Chp. 2.
20. Søren Kierkegaard, *Practice in Christianity*, trans. Howard V. Hong and Edna H. Hong (Princeton: Princeton University Press, 1991) p. 58.
21. *Philosophical Fragments*, p. 101.
22. *Philosophical Fragments*, p. 52.

23. See *Philosophical Fragments*, p. 47.
24. Ibid.
25. *Philosophical Fragments*, p. 37.
26. *Philosophical Fragments*, p. 48.
27. Ibid.
28. Ibid.
29. See *Philosophical Fragments*, pp. 54 and 59, for two different versions of this formula for faith. The translation used here is my own.
30. *Philosophical Fragments*, p. 9.
31. See *Philosophical Fragments*, p. 15 for a discussion of 'the condition'.
32. *Philosophical Fragments*, p. 10.
33. *Philosophical Fragments*, p. 11.
34. Kierkegaard means by 'the Truth' here not just any propositional truth, but the grasping of the Truth that transforms a person; in other words, having Truth in this sense is equivalent to the religious concept of salvation. See Chp. 1 of *Philosophical Fragments*.
35. In Kierkegaard's Danish, all nouns are capitalised. Thus, it is difficult to decide when a noun such as 'Truth' is being used as a proper noun designating a particular kind of truth. In my view, the concepts of Truth and Untruth in *Philosophical Fragments* should be capitalised.
36. *Philosophical Fragments*, p. 14.
37. Ibid.
38. See Emmanuel Levinas, *Totality and Infinity*, trans. Alphonso Lingis (Pittsburgh: Duquesne University Press, 1969), particularly pp. 187–219.
39. Kierkegaard argues this in a lengthy footnote on pp. 16 and 17 in *Philosophical Fragments*.
40. See *Philosophical Fragments*, pp. 27–32.
41. *Philosophical Fragments*, p. 54.
42. *Philosophical Fragments*, 59.
43. *Philosophical Fragments*, p. 54.
44. Robert Adams, 'Kierkegaard's Arguments Against Objective Reasoning in Religion', in *The Virtue of Faith and other Essays in Philosophical Theology* (Oxford: Oxford University Press, 1987) pp. 25–41. Originally published in *The Monist* 60 (1976).
45. Adams, pp. 25–27.
46. *Concluding Unscientific Postscript*, p. 26. (Adams himself, writing before the new Hong translation appeared, cites the old Lowrie-Swenson translation; I here follow the new translation.)
47. Adams, p. 28.
48. Many sections of *Concluding Unscientific Postscript* deal with the nature of the subjective thinker, but one of the central descriptions is found on pp. 349–60, where we have an account of the 'subjective thinker: his task, his form, his style'.
49. See Chp. 3, pp. 47–52.
50. See Chp. 3, pp. 41–7.
51. See my article, 'Kierkegaard and Plantinga on Belief in God: Subjectivity as the Ground of Properly Basic Beliefs', *Faith and Philosophy* (v, 1), 1988.
52. This is exactly what Kierkegaard argues, both in *Philosophical Fragments* and *Concluding Unscientific Postscript*. In both books, he performs thought experiments in which he imagines first that the religious apologist has all the evidence he or she could possibly want, and then that the sceptic has all the negative evidence he or she could want. In both cases Kierkegaard suggests that the results have no decisive importance for faith. See *Fragments*, pp. 58–61, and *Postscript*, pp. 28–31.
53. *Concluding Unscientific Postscript*, p. 211.
54. *Concluding Unscientific Postscript*, p. 231.
55. For a fuller development of this point, as well as a fuller discussion of what is defensible and what is not in Kierkegaard's view of the relation of faith to historical evidence, see Chp. 9 of my *Passionate Reason: Making Sense of Kierkegaard's* Philosophical Fragments (Bloomington, Indiana: Indiana University Press, 1992).
56. For a full account of how historical religious beliefs could be properly basic and yet still vulnerable to defeat by evidence, see my *The Historical Christ and the Jesus of Faith: The Incarnational Narrative as History* (Oxford: Oxford University Press, 1996), especially Chps. 10–12.

8

A Fideistic Account of Knowing God

In the preceding chapters, I have given a general sketch of a responsible fideistic view by focusing on the views of faith and reason held by Aquinas, Kant and Kierkegaard. Aquinas and Kant argue that human reason has limits and that it is reasonable to recognise those limits and the need for a faith that enables one partially to transcend those limitations. Kierkegaard agrees with Aquinas and Kant about the finitude of human reason, but goes further to claim that there is a kind of natural tension between faith and human reason as it is concretely employed.

Human reason is not only finite but defective in ways that require faith (understood to be a gift of grace, since faith is not something humans can achieve on their own) for reason to be healed and function properly so as to obtain essential religious truth. It is possible, however, for reason itself to recognise its own 'neediness', if it is properly 'educated' by a transforming encounter with God's revelation. What I wish to do in the remaining chapters is to explore the implications of such a view of faith and reason for several important areas in the philosophy of religion. Specifically, in this chapter I shall look at the general question of whether there is such a thing as a 'natural' knowledge of God and how such knowledge is possible. In the next two chapters I will look in turn at the question of whether the occurrence of evil makes religious belief irrational and the question as to how an individual might come to have knowledge of specific doctrines of a particular religion. Since Kierkegaard's views have been taken as the prime example of fideism, special attention will be given to his thinking on all three topics.

IS NATURAL KNOWLEDGE OF GOD POSSIBLE AT ALL?

One might think that the fideist position would be simply to deny that any knowledge of God is possible at all. Certainly this is the kind of position that Kant's memorable dictum discussed in Chapter 5 suggests: that one must deny knowledge to make room for faith. Aquinas also seems to define knowledge and faith in mutually exclusive terms. However, both Aquinas and Kant use the term 'knowledge' in rather specialised, technical ways. Aquinas limits *scientia* (usually translated as 'knowledge', but not a strict equivalent to the English term) to cases where a person has a kind of intellectual intuition of truth that is based on an understanding of the universal essence of a thing; to know, a person must 'see' the truth. Much of what we today would accept as scientific knowledge, as well as most ordinary 'common sense' knowledge, would fail to qualify as knowledge by this definition. Kant still holds to the type of epistemology associated with what is today termed 'Enlightenment foundationalism'. This view requires knowledge to be based on evidence that is absolutely clear and compelling. Once more, on such a view a great deal of what is considered knowledge in both ordinary experience and natural science would fail to count as knowledge.[1]

Hence it is not clear that if we have what might be termed a modest, realistic account of knowledge that faith and knowledge must be mutually exclusive. As for Kierkegaard, we shall see that his view is more complex than it first appears. Kierkegaard often speaks of knowledge and faith as mutually exclusive categories. However, to appreciate Kierkegaard's position, we must take account of differences in the object of religious knowledge, as well as make some distinctions between different senses of 'knowledge'.

The English term 'knowledge' can refer to knowledge of a proposition but also to what is sometimes termed 'knowledge by acquaintance'. Many languages actually have different terms for these two kinds of knowledge. Kierkegaard's Danish language is one of those that marks out this distinction by differentiating between *videnskab* (knowledge of propositions or facts) and *kendskab* (knowledge by personal acquaintance). The former kind of knowledge is linked to science, while the second kind is tied more closely to personal experience. We shall see that while Kierkegaard strongly denies that religious knowledge is identical with or the outcome of scientific knowledge, he does affirm the reality of a type of experiential awareness of God.

We must also pay attention to the proper object of religious knowledge for Kierkegaard. As we have noted, Kierkegaard accepts the Christian claim that the ultimate truth about God that is possible for human beings to grasp is found in God's incarnation in Jesus. The incarnation is viewed by him as a paradox that is not only above human reason but against it as well. Faith in it runs up against the sinful pride and selfishness of human reason. Insofar as 'knowledge' is a product of that natural human reason, Kierkegaard naturally denies that there can be such a thing as knowledge of the incarnation. Even in this case, however, faith is made possible by a kind of first-hand encounter with God in Jesus, so there would seem to be something *like* a knowledge by acquaintance that is linked to faith.

However, aside from an awareness of God incarnate, which Kierkegaard would have hesitated to describe as 'knowledge', there is for Kierkegaard knowledge of God in other ways. Clearly, the knowledge of God in Jesus has a kind of ultimate status for Kierkegaard; it is this awareness of God that he thinks makes it possible for humans to be transformed by God so that they can enjoy real communion with God. The 'passion' that makes it possible to know God in this special way is what Kierkegaard calls faith in the strict sense of the term.[2] The special sense of faith that applies only to Christian faith will be discussed at greater length in Chapter 10.

However, Kierkegaard also believes that there is a kind of general, 'natural' awareness of God that is possible for humans. This knowledge is also linked to a kind of faith for Kierkegaard, though it is not faith in the strict sense referred to above, where faith is an awareness of God in the person of Jesus. Rather, the natural awareness of God is linked to faith in a broader and looser sense. Kierkegaard sometimes calls this kind of faith 'Socratic faith', since it presupposes only the kind of moral and spiritual concern that Socrates exemplified.[3] Socratic faith makes possible an awareness of God that is linked to the natural moral and spiritual strivings of humans. Even if this kind of knowledge of God is less than ideal for Kierkegaard, and even though it must be sharply distinguished from the Christian's faith in Jesus, it is still real and valuable.

What I wish to argue is that a fideist does not have to deny that there is any such thing as a natural knowledge of God. What the fideist must deny is that there is any knowledge of God, or at least any worthwhile knowledge, that can be had independently of faith. Such a claim is consistent, however, with affirming the possibility of real knowledge that is dependent on faith.

PROOFS OF GOD'S EXISTENCE AND LOGICAL ARGUMENT

This kind of fideistic view of the knowledge of God can be fleshed out a bit by looking at an account of the often-discussed attempts by philosophers to prove the existence of God. Many different kinds of argument have been advanced, but there are three kinds of arguments that have been more discussed than any others.

Ontological arguments attempt to show that the very idea of God implies that God must exist; one can see that God must be real merely by reflecting on the concept of God. Cosmological arguments claim that God must exist as the ultimate explanation of the universe; some versions of this argument are called 'first-cause' arguments. Teleological arguments try to show that God must exist as the cause of the design or purposive order in the natural world. What should a fideist say about such arguments?

The American philosopher George Mavrodes provides a helpful starting point by distinguishing several different ways arguments in general can be evaluated.[4] One question that may be asked about an argument concerns what logicians call its validity. A valid argument is one in which the conclusion is logically implied by its premises, regardless of whether or not those premises are true. If an argument is valid, then one can say that its conclusion will be true if its premises are true, because that conclusion necessarily follows from those premises. The following argument is valid, though it obviously has false premises:

1. All Martians are green.
2. Jojo is a Martian.
3. Therefore Jojo is green.

A second question concerns the soundness of the argument. An argument is sound if it is both valid and has true premises. One might think that this is all that one could expect of an argument, because a sound argument will have a true conclusion. However, Mavrodes points out that it is quite possible for an argument to be sound but not *known* to be sound by anyone, a feature that obviously detracts from its value. For example, consider the following two arguments, both of which involve a well-known conjecture about prime numbers. Some mathematicians have speculated that there are an infinite number of 'twin primes', which are pairs of prime numbers where the second is 2 larger than the first, such as 3 and 5.

Argument A:

1. If there is a largest pair of twin primes, then there is a pair of primes larger than any other where the second prime is the result of adding 2 to the first prime.
2. There is a largest pair of twin primes.
3. There is a particular pair of primes larger than any other where the second prime is the result of adding 2 to the first prime.

Argument B:

1. If there is a largest pair of twin primes, then there is a pair of primes larger than any other where the second prime is the result of adding 2 to the first prime.
2. It is not the case that there is a largest pair of twin primes.
3. There is no particular pair of primes larger than any other where the second prime is the result of adding 2 to the first prime.

Both arguments are formally valid. Premise 1. in each of these arguments is identical and must be true because it follows from the definition of a twin prime. Premise 2. in one of the arguments is true. Unfortunately, no human knows which is true, because no human knows whether or not there is an infinite number of twin primes, even though if there is, it will be a necessary truth that there is, and if there is not, it will be a necessary truth that there is not. Hence, one of the arguments is sound, but this is not very useful to know, since we do not know which one that is.

Mavrodes points out that there is still more that we can ask of an argument, for it is possible for an argument to be sound, and known to be sound, but still less than helpful as an argument. This is so because it may be that one knows a particular argument is sound only because one already knows the conclusion of the argument to be true. Take, for instance, the following argument:

1. Either God exists or the moon is made of green cheese.
2. It is not the case that the moon is made of green cheese.
3. God exists.

If God exists, then this argument is sound. It is valid in any case. The second premise is true, and if God exists, then the first premise will also be true, since that premise is a disjunction (an 'either-or' proposition) that will be true if either of its disjuncts is true. So if anyone knows that God exists, that person can also know the argument is sound. However, the argument is obviously of no value in extending one's knowledge, if one knows the argument is sound only because one already knows the conclusion. It would seem then that a logical argument would be most useful if it can be known to be sound, and known to be sound without having to know the conclusion in advance.[5]

In such discussions, note that there is a necessary reference to *someone* who knows the soundness of a proof, or knows that soundness in a particular way. This implies that logical arguments have what Mavrodes calls a 'person-relative' character. An argument may be known to be sound by one individual and not by another; may be valuable to one person and not another. In looking at arguments for God's existence, we must therefore ask, 'For whom are such arguments valuable'? These points of Mavrodes are important in looking at what Kierkegaard and other fideists have to say about attempts to prove God's existence.

KIERKEGAARD'S CRITIQUE OF PROOFS OF GOD

Kierkegaard gives a well-known critique of attempts to prove God's existence in Chapter 3 of his book *Philosophical Fragments*. One objection he raises is essentially a claim that such arguments have little worth because they are unnecessary for people of faith and will be regarded as impossible by people who do not have faith. Either God exists or he does not, says Kierkegaard. If God does not exist, then it is impossible to invent a sound argument for his reality, and if I believe that it is true that God does not exist, I will not try to prove that he does. So the only people who will try to prove God's existence will be people who already believe in God, but for such people the proof is unnecessary. With respect to God's existence, Kierkegaard says that 'it is foolishness to want to demonstrate it, since I, in the very moment the proof begins would presuppose it . . . as decided'.[6]

Kierkegaard is not claiming that sound arguments for God's existence cannot be developed, but raising a critical question: For whom are these arguments valuable? However, though Kierkegaard is probably correct to maintain that only people who already believe in God will try to construct an argument for God's reality, it does not seem to follow that such arguments are always without value. The argument might still be convincing to someone other than the person who constructed the argument. Also, even for someone who already believes, it is conceivable that such an argument could have the value of strengthening the person's belief by helping the individual to see its ground more clearly.

Perhaps Kierkegaard does not see this objection as decisive either, for he goes on to give some more specific objections to particular arguments. The ontological argument claims to show that God must exist because God is by definition the most perfect being and must have all perfections, including the perfection of existence. Kierkegaard rejects this argument for the same reason that many other philosophers have given. He maintains that it is not possible to determine what exists in reality simply by thinking about definitions. We may if we wish define God as a being who necessarily exists, but this does not mean that God exists, but only that if he does, the kind of existence he has would be necessary existence. The ontological argument expresses a 'profound tautology' but a tautology cannot give us any information about what exists as a matter of fact.[7]

Kierkegaard also gives an interesting critique of the teleological argument or argument from design. As he sees this argument, it involves an attempt to infer the existence of God from the observation of 'the wisdom in nature and the goodness or wisdom in Governance'.[8] It is true that we can properly see the works of God as pointing to God's reality, says Kierkegaard. The difficulty lies in recognising the works of God in the natural world as the works of God:

> [A]re the wisdom in nature and the goodness or wisdom in Governance right in front of our noses? Do we not encounter the most terrible spiritual trials here, and is it ever possible to be finished with all these trials?[9]

Kierkegaard's claim is that our experience of the natural world is ambiguous. It is possible to see the natural world as the product of a good God, but there is also much in nature that is disturbing and hard to reconcile with seeing it as the outcome of the work of a supremely good God. The person who finds such a proof convincing, according to Kierkegaard, begins not with an immediate experience of indubitable fact, but with an 'ideal interpretation' of his experience. In effect, the person begins by interpreting the natural world as God's handiwork; only on this basis does the individual dare to 'defy all objections, even those that have not yet arisen'.[10]

If this is so, then it is not the proof that is the basis of the person's faith in God. It is rather the person's faith in God, which guides the interpretation, that is the basis of the proof. In beginning the proof I presuppose that God exists and actually begin with trust in him.[11] If this were not so and my faith in God really rested on the proof, then I 'would be obliged continually to live in suspense lest something so terrible happen that my fragment of demonstration would be ruined'.[12] Some post-Holocaust thinkers have claimed that this 'something so terrible' has in fact occurred.

Strictly speaking, this is not an objection to giving arguments for God's existence; it is only an objection to thinking that such arguments can have value independently of faith. In fact, Kierkegaard credits Socrates with the invention of the teleological argument, and as Socrates is one of his intellectual and spiritual heroes, it seems likely that he would not object to such arguments so long as they are not seen as a substitute for faith.

What is faith here and what value does an argument have if recognising its soundness depends on faith? For Kierkegaard, faith in God in the general sense we are here discussing (which must, it should be remembered, be contrasted with faith in the special sense of faith in the incarnation) is essentially a developed spiritual capacity. Cognitively this capacity expresses itself by giving a person an interpretive skill, an ability to see a pattern and discern its meaning, where those who lack the skill in question might see nothing.

Kierkegaard calls faith in all its forms a 'passion' and he means by this not a momentary feeling, but a long-term emotion. He often illustrates faith by comparing it to love, not the momentary passion of someone who is infatuated, but the developed, 'formed' disposition of the true lover. One of the characteristics of a person who genuinely loves another is a heightened sensitivity, an ability to recognise the good qualities of the loved one. In an analogous way, a person of faith, a kind of lover of God who has developed the capacity to trust God, has a heightened capacity to see God's presence. Just as a lover knows how to interpret the behaviour of the beloved, so the person of faith knows how to interpret the handiwork of God seen about us.

A Kierkegaardian may therefore see some arguments for God's existence as attempts to articulate and make clearer what I would call signs or pointers to God's presence. Without the heightened sensitivities that faith provides one cannot properly recognise and appreciate those divine signs and pointers. Nevertheless, the signs and pointers thus recognised might be quite real and could function as reliable indicators of God's reality.[13]

Many of the philosophical discussions of arguments for God's existence seem to presuppose a particular kind of epistemology. According to this view, for an argument to be a good one, it must be based on premises that are acceptable to nearly everyone. Good arguments start from evidence that is universally available and objectively certain. Kierkegaard and other fideists would reject the demand to develop arguments for God's existence that meet this standard.

The kind of epistemology that underlies this demand for universality seems dubious. I am not 'everyone'; I am a particular individual. I know things that some other people do not know, and do not know things that other people know. Hence, an argument that is convincing to me may not be convincing to another and vice versa. Many arguments that reasonable people find persuasive in politics and economics do not meet the standard of being based on premises that are universally accepted. Even in natural science, it is increasingly recognised that evidence is only evidence for people who approach the data with the right 'paradigm' or 'conceptual scheme' or have developed the capacity to see things in a particular way by being socialised into a scientific community.[14] Hence in principle it seems open to a fideist to hold that there is evidence for God's reality that could be articulated in arguments, but also that this evidence can only be recognised by people who have actualised the capacities that come with the development of faith.[15]

Perhaps it is helpful to draw a distinction between an intellectual inquiry that is 'algorithmic' and one that essentially involves 'hermeneutics' or interpretation. An algorithmic process is one that can be objectively specified in steps that can be followed precisely. If you have an algorithm for a math problem, then you have a procedure that guarantees a solution in a finite number of steps if properly followed. Intellectual tasks such as explaining the meaning of a book cannot be algorithmic in character, because interpretation does not seem to be an activity that can be broken down into a series of clear and distinct operations.

How do we learn the meaning of a book? Basically, by reading it. As we read, we have some initial ideas about what the book is about (what some have called a 'pre-understanding'). As we begin to read we develop a sense of what the book is saying, and our overall sense is modified as we read further. Sometimes our initial ideas are confirmed and refined as we read; sometimes we change our ideas drastically. However, different people, who approach the book with different sets of questions and assumptions, will certainly give somewhat different accounts of what the book is saying. People differ in both their pre-understandings and in their interpretive skills. Yet this is not a process in which anything goes; not all interpretations are equally valid. One may question whether St Paul's *Epistle to the Romans* is more centrally concerned with justification by faith or with the continued place of the Hebrew people in God's plan, but no reasonable person can say the book is primarily about the value of public ownership of the means of production.

Frequently, the problem of interpretation focuses on what is known as the 'hermeneutical circle'. The difficulty is this. To understand a particular passage in a text one must have some sense of the meaning of the text as a whole. However, it appears that one can only get a sense of the text as a whole by reading (and understanding) particular texts. This hermeneutical circle cannot be so great a problem that people find it impossible to read and understand books, because we know that they do. The solution is simply to recognise that reading and understanding is an on-going process, where our readings of the particular are always shaped by our understanding of the whole, but where our understanding of the whole is always being tested and refined by our reading and understanding of particular passages.[16]

I think it is clear that religious questions are among those that are hermeneutical rather than algorithmic. Hence, it is not surprising that religious knowledge is heavily dependent on the convictions and skills that people bring with them to the enterprise. And to speak of those convictions and skills is to speak of faith. There may be no intellectual inquiry into religious questions that is not shaped by faith. However, this does not mean that faith cannot be honestly tested, just as reading a book can provide an honest test for a particular interpretation of the book.

EXPERIENTIAL AWARENESS OF GOD

In speaking of the role of faith in making possible an awareness of signs or pointers to God's reality, we have already begun to discuss religious experience. Within the general framework of religious experience, a distinction must be drawn between experiences that may be interpreted religiously and religious experiences of God in a strict sense. There are many people who find religious meaning in an experience of a sunset or childbirth, but people who have such experiences do not necessarily think they are directly experiencing God. What does Kierkegaard, as a representative fideist, think about the possibility of experiencing God?

Kierkegaard's view on this issue is once again complex and subtle. If by 'experience of God' we mean some immediate experience, especially some sensory experience that anyone can have regardless of degree of religious and moral sensitivity, Kierkegaard denies that there is any experience of God. The claim that God can be *directly* experienced is characterised by Kierkegaard as 'paganism', even though most of the 'pagans' he describes are actually part of Christendom.[17] 'All paganism consists in this, that god is related directly to a human being, as the remarkably striking to the amazed'.[18] Kierkegaard satirises this kind of 'pagan' in a memorable passage. He imagines a person who lives within Christendom but lacks any sense of living his life 'before God'. Instead, he simply looks around to see how 'the others' live:

> At the end of his life, one would have to say that one thing had escaped him: he had not become aware of God. If God could have permitted a direct relationship, he would certainly have become aware. If God had taken the form, for example, of a rare, enormously large green bird, with a red beak, that perched in a tree on the embankment and perhaps even whistled in an unprecedented manner – then our partygoing man would surely have had his eyes opened; for the first time in his life he would have been able to be the first.[19]

While denying that this type of 'direct' awareness of God is possible, Kierkegaard insists just as strongly that a person who is spiritually and morally developed can be aware of God's presence. For Kierkegaard, God is indeed present within creation, but he is present in an illusive form and cannot be directly observed.[20] '[W]ithin the individual human being there is a possibility (he is spirit according to his possibility) that in inwardness is awakened to a God-relationship, and then it is possible to see God everywhere.'[21]

This is not the result of an arbitrary decision on God's part, but a necessary consequence of God's own character. The problem with God taking the form of the large green bird is that the person who becomes aware of God in that form would not really become aware of God *as God*, and hence would not discover what God is actually like. The requirement of 'like can only be known by like' means that to know God as a spiritual, moral power, it is necessary for the individual to become spiritually and morally developed.

It is not accidental that Kierkegaard connects spiritual development with moral development, for he belongs in the tradition of those thinkers who see human conscience as the voice of God.[22] Kierkegaard is very well aware of the historical relativity of human moral thinking. The particular content of my moral conscience is heavily shaped by the moral community in which I have been socialised. Nevertheless, in and through this relativity, Kierkegaard thinks that the *form* of the moral life still reveals something true: human beings are creatures of God and we are responsible to God for how we live our lives. Authentic individuals ought to think of themselves as 'standing before God' in all that they do. Amid the historical relativities of my moral situation, I am still faced with decisions in which a choice for good or evil must be made. The religious life begins when an individual recognises both the seriousness of that choice and the responsibility it involves. As the person develops, the task of 'standing before God' is seen as requiring an answer to the universal human problems of suffering and guilt.[23] However much Kierkegaard as a Christian may stress the vital character of knowing God in the form of the man Jesus of Nazareth, he also affirms that there is a type of awareness of God potentially present in all human beings as they become aware of what he calls 'the eternal' dimension to their lives.

Hence, with respect to experiential awareness of God, the fideist may say something similar to what was said about theistic arguments. The possibility of a natural knowledge of God that is independent of faith is denied. God cannot be known in just any old circumstances by anyone; there is no experiential awareness of him that is immediately and universally available. Natural religious knowledge is dependent on faith, and faith here refers to the spiritual sensitivities and capacities that are the precondition of truly knowing God. The fideistic denial that there is any 'neutral' knowledge of God independent of faith is consistent with an affirmation that when faith is present, a real acquaintance with God is possible.

NOTES

1. For a clear discussion and critique of various forms of foundationalism in philosophy of religion, see Kelly James Clark, *Return to Reason* (Grand Rapids, Michigan: Wm B. Eerdmans, 1990), especially pp. 123–43.
2. The distinction is drawn in *Philosophical Fragments*, p. 87. See the discussion of this in Chapter 6, pp. 86–8.
3. For a discussion of Socratic faith, see *Concluding Unscientific Postscript*, trans. Howard V. and Edna H. Hong (Princeton: Princeton University Press, 1992) pp. 206n–7n.
4. See George Mavrodes, *Belief in God* (New York: Random House, 1970) pp. 17–48.
5. An argument that did not meet this requirement might still have some usefulness, by exhibiting logical relations, for example.
6. Søren Kierkegaard, *Philosophical Fragments*, trans. Howard V. and Edna H. Hong (Princeton: Princeton University Press, 1985) p. 39. (translation modified).
7. See Kierkegaard, *Philosophical Fragments*, pp. 41n–2n. For a rigorous defence of a version of the ontological argument, see Alvin Plantinga, *God, Freedom, and Evil* (Grand Rapids, Michigan: Wm B. Eerdmans, 1977) pp. 85–112.
8. Kierkegaard, *Philosophical Fragments*, p. 42.
9. Ibid.
10. Ibid.
11. Ibid.
12. Ibid.
13. For a discussion of theistic arguments that interprets them as such 'natural signs' that require faith to be read properly, see my *Why Believe? Reason and Mystery as Pointers to God* (Grand Rapids, Michigan: Wm B. Eerdmans, 1996)
14. For the classic defence of this view, see Thomas Kuhn, *The Structure of Scientific Revolutions*, 2nd edn (Chicago: University of Chicago Press, 1970). Kuhn's ideas are sometimes understood as implying some kind of relativism, but his historical theses can be accepted without accepting any such relativism. For a balanced account of the nature of scientific method, see Del Ratzsch, *Philosophy of Science: The Natural Sciences in Christian Perspective* (Downers Grove, Illinois: InterVarsity Press, 1986).
15. See Kelly Clark, *Return to Reason*, Chp. 1, for an argument for a similar view.
16. For more on the hermeneutical dimension of religious questions, see my *Philosophy of Religion: Thinking About Faith* (Downers Grove, Illinois: InterVarsity Press, 1985) pp. 166–79.
17. Kierkegaard, *Concluding Unscientific Postscript*, pp. 243–5.
18. Kierkegaard, *Concluding Unscientific Postscript*, p. 245.
19. Ibid.
20. Kierkegaard, *Concluding Unscientific Postscript*, p. 243.
21. Kierkegaard, *Concluding Unscientific Postscript*, pp. 246–47.
22. Søren Kierkegaard, *The Sickness Unto Death*, trans. Howard V. and Edna H. Hong (Princeton: Princeton University Press, 1980) p. 124.
23. See the long discussion of suffering and guilt as the 'essential' and 'decisive' forms of the natural religious life that Kierkegaard calls 'Religiousness A' in *Concluding Unscientific Postscript*, pp. 431–55.
24. For an interesting account of views that stress the idea that the evidence for religious belief requires some kind of passional transformation of the individual in order to be recognised, see William J. Wainwright, *Reason and the Heart: A Prolegomenon to a Critique of Passional Reason* (Ithaca, New York: Cornell University Press, 1995).

9

Faith and the Problem of Evil

Some philosophers have attempted to prove God's existence, as we saw in the previous chapter. However, others have tried to do just the opposite; they have tried to show that God does not or even could not exist. The most serious arguments against the reality of God have taken as their starting point the evil and suffering that is so pervasive in this world. A God who is both completely powerful and knowledgeable, as traditional theists have conceived God, would seem to be able to prevent evil from occurring. A God who is completely good and loving would want to do that, or so it is claimed by many philosophers. So if God exists, there should be no evil at all. Yet it is clear that 'bad stuff happens', as my colleague Steve Wykstra fetchingly states the problem of evil.[1]

This problem is much discussed in philosophy of religion. In this chapter I shall try to see what light can be shed on it by the kind of perspective on faith and reason we have been examining. Can a view that makes faith central to religious knowledge and emphasises the limitations of human reason help in understanding why God allows evil? Can such a perspective help decide the question as to whether evil makes religious faith unreasonable?

THE LOGICAL FORM OF THE PROBLEM OF EVIL

The problem of evil comes in many different forms. The most serious charge made by atheistic philosophers is that evil constitutes a *disproof* of God's existence, because it is logically contradictory to assert both the existence of God as traditionally conceived (a being perfect in power, knowledge and goodness) and the occurrence of evil. A classical formulation of this form of the problem is provided in an article by J. L. Mackie.[2] In addition to the classical definition of God as possessing the three perfections just mentioned, Mackie's argument relies on two principles that he calls 'quasi-logical rules': 'that good is opposed to evil, in such a way that a good thing always eliminates evil as far as it can, and that there are no limits to what an omnipotent being can do'.[3] As Mackie sees it, the three propositions 'God is omnipotent; God is wholly good; and yet evil exists' are contradictory, yet all three are essential to theistic belief. 'The theologian, it seems, at once *must* adhere and *cannot consistently* adhere to all three'.[4]

Such a charge is one that must be taken seriously, even by fideists. For fideism, at least as I have interpreted it, does not wish faith to come into conflict with logical truths and cannot simply embrace genuine logical contradictions.[5] Nor can the believer simply assume without argument that reason is completely powerless when it comes to looking at religious questions. A rebuttal of this kind of attack on faith therefore still seems to be needed for someone who adopts a fideistic perspective. For even if fideists are not sympathetic to positive attempts to prove the truth of religion, they may still seek flaws in attempts to prove that their religious beliefs are untrue. And the fideist thinks the prospects for success in such an enterprise are good, since the very limitations of reason that make positive proof, or at least proof that is supposed to be independent of faith, difficult or impossible would also seem to make any proof of falsehood difficult or impossible as well.

Fortunately, what is often called the 'atheological' argument from evil is far from conclusive, and the critiques of this argument seem quite consistent with characteristic fideist themes.[6] To criticise Mackie's version of the argument, I shall first examine his assumption that a good being always eliminates all the evil that it can.

This principle, far from being a necessary truth, seems downright false, unless it is significantly qualified. There are lots of evils that could be but are not prevented by good beings. If parents never allowed their teenage children to ride in automobiles, certain kinds of dangers the children are exposed to would be eliminated, and in the long run some evils that will occur would be prevented. No teenagers would be involved in road accidents. However, most people would not agree that parents have an obligation to adopt such a policy (though some might think it permissible). The problem of course is that the policy would eliminate some evils, but also eliminate many goods and probably create other evils as well. (In an emergency, for example, a child who was not allowed to ride in a car might not receive prompt medical care.) It is not correct, then, to say that go-

people will always eliminate any evils they can. What is more plausible is to say that a person will eliminate an evil except where eliminating that evil would prevent a greater good or create a greater evil.

One may rightly point out, of course, that there is a vast difference between a human parent and God. Finite human beings are greatly limited in their ability to eliminate evils without eliminating greater goods or creating greater evils because of the limitations of their power and knowledge. Surely, the atheist may argue, God is not limited in the same way.

God's power and knowledge certainly must vastly exceed that of any human agent. The fideist, as we shall later see, insists on this and makes good use of it in responding to the problem of evil. However, even though God must be very great, it is not at all obvious that Mackie's 'quasi-logical rule' that there are no limits to what an omnipotent being can do is correct. If this principle is not correct, then it is not at all clear that even God can eliminate all evils without losing any greater goods or creating any greater evils. Obviously, philosophical reflection here must centre on the question of what it means to be all-powerful. Are there any limitations at all to what an all-powerful being can do?

Most philosophers of religion have traditionally held that even an omnipotent being cannot do what is logically impossible. God could not, for example, create a stone that was not a stone, because such a feat requires him to create a logically contradictory state of affairs. Furthermore, it is often argued that certain kinds of goods and evils are logically linked together. Physical courage, for example, might be defined as a willingness to suffer physical pain or even death for the sake of doing what is believed to be right. If such a definition is accepted, then not even God could create a world in which physical courage exists unless that world also included physical pain.

Of course, physical courage is not the only kind of goodness that might require God to allow some evils. Moral goodness is a specially important kind of goodness according to many thinkers. Some, such as Immanuel Kant, have claimed that it is only moral goodness that is absolutely and unconditionally good.[7] Others would not go so far as Kant, but almost veryone would agree that moral goodness is tremendously significant. ppose that moral freedom is logically required in order for humans to ess moral goodness, so that a robot who always appeared to act in lly good ways but who had no freedom of choice would lack moral ss in any deep sense. Suppose also, as seems plausible to many, that moral freedom requires that the possessor be able to misuse that dom to choose evil. In that case it would seem that it would be logically impossible for God to create a world in which there is moral goodness without that world also containing the possibility of moral evil.[8]

The atheist may here wonder whether these claims about the nature of moral goodness are true. However, even if the claims about moral goodness and the value of free will cannot be securely established, the atheistic argument from evil is in trouble. The atheist is making a strong claim, a claim that the existence of God can be disproved by the occurrence of evil, which is a claim that requires that we *know* that the existence of God and the occurrence of evil are logically incompatible. However, if we have cause to wonder whether or not God might have good reasons to allow evil, if it even seems *possible* that a good God might allow evil in order to create a world with certain goods in it, then the argument is undermined. For the atheological argument to work, the atheist must be sure that there are no goods that could require God to allow evil, but it is hard to see how the atheist could be sure about this.

Responses by theists to the problem of evil are sometimes divided into *theodicies* and *defences*. A theodicy is an attempt to explain why God allows evil, to give the reasons why a perfectly good, all-powerful being would allow evil to occur. A defence is a more modest enterprise, which simply tries to give reasons a good God might have for allowing evil, or argues that it is reasonable to believe that God has reasons, even if we do not know what those reasons are. The above rebuttal rests only on a defence, not a theodicy, since in it I only gave possible reasons why God might allow (at least some) evils. The fideist is attracted to the defence strategy, because fideists think that human beings may not be capable of actually understanding God well enough to grasp his actual reasons.

Therefore, in a rebuttal to the atheologian's argument, the fideist emphasis on the limitations of reason may be salutary. A strategy of defence seems more suited to our actual human cognitive capacities. Furthermore, a defence seems all that is necessary for intellectually responsible faith. Though we humans may well wish we had a theodicy, our wishes cannot dictate what must be the case to reality. As an intelligent layperson, I may think I should be able to understand contemporary physics, and I may wish that quantum mechanics were simpler and easier to understand than it is, but reality (and physics) take no notice of my cognitive limitations.

In the same way, if God is real, then the nature of his reality cannot be regarded as subject to the limitations of my intellect. When human reason attempts to understand God and think through such concepts as omnipotence and perfect goodness, it is operating outside of its natural element. As we saw in Chapters 4–6, many philosophers have argued that God is at least above human reason. We humans are not God and we have no experience of perfect goodness in our experiences with each other. The fideist says that to know God properly, we must have a relationship to God based on faith as trust. Without such a relationship, our insights into God's character are scanty and flimsy. It is not that we have no idea at all what a perfectly good and all-powerful being would be like; it is rather that our insights are limited and our inferences about what God must be like must be cautious. Even with faith, our knowledge of God is sharply limited; without faith it is modest indeed.

Of course if reason has the kind of imperialistic character we discussed in looking at Kierkegaard in Chapter 7, then reason will not be inclined to recognise its limitations and may become angry and contemptuous about claims that reason is limited. The fideist finds such a reaction understandable and so is not intimidated by this imperialistic bluster. The fideist calmly insists that we human beings are not God. Such a perspective puts a limit on apologetic arguments, as we saw in the previous chapter, since the fideist denies that any proofs of God can be given that operate independently of faith. However, the fideist perspective also limits the pretensions of the opponents of religious belief. It looks as though opponents of religious belief would have to know far more than it is possible for humans to know in order to prove that God does not exist.

THE EVIDENTIAL FORM OF THE PROBLEM OF EVIL

The atheologian may be able to regroup and mount an attack from a slightly different direction. He may be forced to concede that we cannot know that God's existence and the occurrence of evil are logically incompatible states of affairs. It is possible that a good God who is all-powerful might allow evils for the sake of certain great goods. However, the atheologian may question whether it is likely or probable that there are such goods. If this is improbable, then even if evil does not logically disprove God's existence, it might still count as strong evidence against God's reality. Arguments along this line make up what is often called the evidential form of the problem of evil.

An evidential line of attack may focus not simply on the mere occurrence of evil, but also on the quantity, quality and character of the evil and suffering around us. The atheologian asks whether or not the actual world, with its horrible earthquakes and tornadoes, its cancer and heart disease, its appalling accidents and gruesome crimes, is the kind of world we would expect a powerful good God to create. It seems very probable, the atheologian may reason, that no great goods would be lost if God were to relieve some of this suffering and make the world a significantly better place than it is. So even if evil does not disprove God's existence, it surely counts as evidence against God's reality, evidence strong enough to make belief in God unreasonable.

A clear example of the evidential form of the problem of evil is found in the work of William Rowe.[9] The key premise in Rowe's argument is the following: 'There exist instances of intense suffering which an omnipotent, omniscient being could have prevented without thereby losing some greater good or permitting some evil equally bad or worse'.[10] Since Rowe thinks that an all-powerful, perfectly good being would not allow such instances of suffering, if this premise can be established, we have a powerful argument against belief in God's existence.

Why does Rowe think that this premise is true? He begins with a case of animal suffering:

> Suppose in some distant forest lightning strikes a dead tree, resulting in a forest fire. In the fire a fawn is trapped, horribly burned, and lies in terrible agony for several days before death relieves its suffering. So far as we can see the fawn's intense suffering is pointless. For there does not appear to be any greater good such that the prevention of the fawn's suffering would require either the loss of that good or the occurrence of an evil equally bad or worse.[11]

Now Rowe admits that the fact that we cannot see what good might be served by the fawn's suffering does not prove that there is no such good. Perhaps there is some good, familiar or unfamiliar to us, that we just don't know about. However, he takes it that the fact that the fawn's suffering *appears* to be pointless constitutes evidence that it is. And of course there are numerous examples of suffering similar to the fawn in seeming to be, for all we can tell, pointless. It is possible that all of these do in fact serve some point, but to Rowe this seems quite unlikely. Given the fact that these evils do not appear to serve any good purpose, we can conclude that the key premise (that there are instances of suffering God could have prevented without losing any greater good or causing any comparable or greater evil), though not provable, is 'altogether *reasonable* to believe'.[12]

Stephen Wykstra has responded to Rowe by making heavy use of a key fideistic theme, the limitations of human knowledge in comparison to God.[13] As Wykstra sees it, the key move in Rowe's argument is an inference that goes something like this: from 'It appears there is no purpose served by many evils' one infers that 'It is reasonable to believe there is no purpose served by many evils'.[14] Such an inference is not inherently fallacious; it is rather similar in form to what is sometimes called the 'principle of credulity', which is simply the principle that if things appear to be such and such, then that fact provides at least some reason to think they are such and such. Of course we all know that appearances can be deceiving, but one might say that we are entitled to believe things are as they appear to be unless we have some reason to think otherwise.

Wykstra thinks that to be acceptable this principle of 'appears so, therefore probably is so' must be qualified. He presents the following kinds of cases to illustrate the kind of qualification that must be added. In case one, a person looks through a doorway into a room full of very large, opaque objects and says there does not appear to be a table in the room. In case two, a person has a bad cold that completely undermines her sense of smell. After smelling some milk that might be sour, she notes that it does not appear to her to be sour. In case three, a professor of ceramics, who knows no philosophy, listens to a philosophy lecture and says that the sentences do not appear to have any clear meaning.[15]

In all three of these cases, it would be rash to reason that things are the way they appear. Or, to be more precise, it would be rash for the subject to claim that things even appear a certain way. It is true that no table appears to the subject (in the first example), but there surely is a difference between the situation where no table appears to me and the situation where there appears to be no table. In this case a table might be present in the room, sitting unseen behind some large object. The milk might be sour, but the sourness undetectable by the defective sense of smell. The sentences of the philosophy lecture might be perfectly sensible, but not understandable to the person who knows no philosophy.

From these examples, Wykstra draws a condition that must be added to the principle of 'appears so, therefore probably is so' to make the principle acceptable. He calls this condition CORNEA, the 'Condition of Reasonable Epistemic Access'.[16] In all three cases examined above, the individual is not justified in holding that things appear in a certain way such that belief that things are that way is justified, because the individual knows that even if things were different, he or she could not expect the appearances to be any different than they are. If there were a table behind some large object, the person will not be able to see it. If the milk were sour, the person would not be able to detect it by smelling. If the philosopher's talk were meaningful, the hearer would still not be able to understand it. The official definition of CORNEA is as follows:

> On the basis of cognized situation s, human H is entitled to claim 'It appears that p' only if it is reasonable for H to believe that, given her cognitive faculties and the use she has made of them, if p were not the case, s would likely be different than it is in some way discernible by her.[17]

Now how does CORNEA bear on Rowe's evidential argument from evil? Suppose that there are goods for the sake of which God allows the kinds of evils Rowe discusses. The question to raise is obviously this: If this is so, is it likely that it would appear to us that there are such goods? If not – if we think that whether there are or are not such goods, things would appear pretty much the same to us – then CORNEA is not satisfied, and we are not justified in concluding from the fact that we do not see any purposes being served by these evils that there probably are no such purposes.

Because of the great superiority of God to humans, Wykstra thinks that we have good reason to doubt whether or not we could detect God's purposes in allowing evil if God is in fact justified in allowing these evils. The difference between the 'vision and wisdom' of God and that of humans is 'roughly as an adult human's is to a one-month-old infant'.[18] It is obvious that such an infant is unlikely to be able to discern most of the purposes of the child's mother. In the same way, it is unlikely that a human being could discern the purposes of an omniscient being. Hence, our failure to detect any such purposes does not really count as strong evidence that there are no such purposes. We here can see in Wykstra's response to Rowe how the characteristic fideist emphasis on the limits of human reason and the ways God exceeds our comprehension of him can undermine the evidential form of the problem of evil.[19]

Perhaps Wykstra's argument can be seen as an instance of one typical fideist response to evidential arguments, though not the only one, in which the fideist attempts to unmask the arguments as resting on a presumptuous attempt to claim that human beings can see reality from a god's-eye point of view. How, the fideist will ask, do we know enough about God and creation to be able to tell what is probable or likely in this case? How do we know that evil counts as evidence against God, and if it does, how can we determine the strength of that evidence? One way of looking at some evidential arguments from evil is to see them as making a claim that the world does not look as I myself would expect it to look if it were created by a good God.[20] But what does this mean? Does it mean that if I were God and had created the world, I would have created a different world? Who am I to make such a claim? I do not wish to suggest that we have no idea as to what one might reasonably expect the world to be like if there is a God, but only that any expectations we do have must be held very tentatively, as befitting their speculative character and our own limitations.

What do I really know about universe-making? In the book of *Job* in the Old Testament, God answers Job out of the whirlwind and questions his credentials to question God: 'Where were you when I laid the foundation of the earth'?[21] Job's reply acknowledges his limitations: 'Therefore I have uttered what I did not understand, things too wonderful for me, which I did not know'.[22]

The limits of human reason sharply limit our ability to develop convincing theodicies. However, the fideist does not see this inability to construct a theodicy as devastating to his or her religious beliefs but as natural and understandable. Suppose it is true that I do not know why God allows evil. What follows? It does not follow that God has no good reason for allowing evil unless I am willing to claim that the following principle is true: If God had a good reason for allowing evil, I would know what that reason is. The fideist claims we have no reason to think this principle is true; in fact, we have good reason to think it is false.

There are other elements in fideism that could also be exploited to deal with the problem of evil. One strategy would be to draw on the 'no-neutrality thesis' that many fideists find attractive. The problem of evil is typically based on an assumption that believers and unbelievers agree on what counts as a good (and an evil) and what kind of good would be required to justify an evil. However, it is not clear that theists and atheists really agree on these things. Nor is it even clear that theists must necessarily accept the claim that God is a moral agent subject to the kinds of obligations that human moral agents are subject to. Many of the arguments from evil seem to presuppose that God is subject to obligations to prevent evils of various kinds because we think that humans are subject to such obligations. However, it is not clear that God's obligations are the same as ours, if he has obligations at all.[23]

EVIL AND THE STRUGGLE OF FAITH

None of this means that evil is not a problem for the person of faith, and it certainly does not mean that fideists must ignore this problem. The fideist should recognise that much of the evil in the world is puzzling and disturbing. The claim of the atheologian that the world does not look as we would expect it to look if created by a God often *feels* right. How, then can we continue to believe in God in such a world?

The fideist answer is of course 'by faith'. However, it is important to be clear about what faith means. It does not mean merely closing one's eyes to difficulties, a blind leap into the dark, or belief with no foundation at all. Faith is a response of trust to a God who has made himself known in some way. There are of course a number of ways religious people believe that God has made himself known. Some believe that God's presence can be experienced in the natural world, or at least that the natural world can be experienced as God's handiwork. Others emphasise the presence of God within the self, particularly when the individual reflects on his or her struggle to grow morally and spiritually. Others say that God primarily makes himself known through prophets and inspired sacred writings, such as the Hebrew Bible (for Jews) or the Koran (for Muslims). Christians of course believe that God has made himself known most fully in the life of Jesus of Nazareth.

However God has made himself known, fideists think that faith is one of the conditions for recognising God's presence. Faith may be seen both as a receptiveness to meeting God, a willingness to look for his presence, and as the trusting response of someone who has made God's acquaintance. Whatever the ground of faith may be, its primary characteristic, as we saw in Chapter 1, is trust.

The question of how belief deals with evil is basically the question as to how it is possible to trust God. Here it is helpful to look at cases of trust in human relationships, which are at least faintly analogous to the relation to God. We can see immediately that trust is compatible with a certain ambiguity in what we might call our evidential situation. Suppose I have a friend who has promised to help me do a job. At the appointed hour my friend does not appear to help me. If I immediately form a belief that my friend has callously ignored her promise, I do not trust my friend very much, if at all. True faith in my friend requires me to consider other hypotheses: perhaps she has been unavoidably detained. The very nature of faith as trust requires that it be able to withstand a certain amount of pressure; faith shows itself to be faith precisely in this kind of testing.

Consider another example. Suppose I am at home preparing dinner. My wife is commuting from another city. I have everything prepared at the appointed hour, but she does not appear. Where is she? I do not know. There are various possibilities. She could have had an accident. Perhaps she was detained at her job. For all I know about the facts in the case, she could have stopped at a roadside tavern, met a strange man and gone off with him. I do not seriously consider the last possibility. Why not? It is not because I know the reason why she has not come home. I do not know and my ignorance distresses me. However, if I have faith in her – if I trust her – I believe she has a good reason for not coming, even without knowing what that reason is. I do not regard my faith as unreasonable, even though it might be regarded as unreasonable by someone else who might cynically tell me that 'smart' people never trust anyone else. An outsider who does not understand my trust or its ground might dismiss my faith as naive and foolish. However, my faith has a ground. Simply put, that ground is my knowledge of my wife. Years of a loving life together have created a foundation of trust.

The fideist finds certain analogies between this case and faith in God in a world that contains evil and suffering. When I look around at the world, a lot of 'bad stuff' indeed happens, and much of the time I do not understand the reasons why it happens. I would like to know; my ignorance distresses me. The occurrence of evil and suffering is for me a problem, a problem that tests my faith. However, if my faith is strong, it will pass the test. Perhaps even if it is weak, the testing process will have value. My faith may be purified, forced to develop. If I have come to know God as good and loving, and have come to trust him, I will believe that God has reasons for allowing evil and suffering, even if I do not know what those reasons are or understand them if I do.

The person who lacks this faith may well find my trust in God naive and foolish. According to the fideist what such a person may need is not primarily intellectual argument (though such arguments might be helpful) but to experience the love and goodness of God, to have the kind of encounter with God that can be the ground of faith. That awareness of God might come in many forms. However, as we have seen, for Christians the knowledge of God is found most fully and clearly in Jesus of Nazareth.

The other great theistic religions have their own ways of responding to the problem of evil, but for Christians the story of Jesus has special power in relation to this issue. For the life of Jesus is essentially a story of suffering, climaxed by a cruel death and then victory over death. Christians believe that Jesus is more than a prophet; he is God himself, assuming the human condition. The story of Jesus contains no theodicy, so far as I can see. There is no theoretical account of why God allows evil. But it does provide assurances of God's love and compassion, and this is a very valuable kind of assurance. It is the assurance of the God who cares enough about his world to share in the sufferings of his fallen creatures. And it is also a demonstration of how God can bring good out of evil and provide victory over both moral evil and death. Such a demonstration is hardly a proof that God will bring good out of all the evils that he permits, but it can strengthen the *faith* of those who know and love God that he can and will do so.

NOTES

1. Though he has not used the phrase 'bad stuff happens' in print, Wykstra is one of the most acute contemporary writers on the subject of the problem of evil. His work is discussed later in this chapter.
2. J. L. Mackie, 'Evil and Omnipotence', in Marilyn McCord Adams and Robert Merrihew Adams, eds, *The Problem of Evil* (Oxford: Oxford University Press, 1990) pp. 25–37. Reprinted from *Mind* 64, 254 (April 1955).
3. Mackie, p. 26.
4. Mackie, p. 25.
5. See Chapter 2, pp. 19–22.
6. For one of the best-known critiques of the logical form of the problem of evil, see Alvin Plantinga, *God, Freedom and Evil* (Grand Rapids, Michigan: Wm B. Eerdmans, 1977).

7. See Kant's claim that 'there is no possibility of thinking of anything at all in the world, or even out of it, which can be regarded as good without qualification, except a *good will*', *Grounding for the Metaphysics of Morals*, p. 7.
8. For a vigorous and rigorous defence of this 'free will argument' against Mackie's attack, see Alvin Plantinga, *The Nature of Necessity* (Oxford: Oxford University Press, 1974), Chp. 9. (Reprinted in Adams and Adams, eds, *The Problem of Evil*.)
9. William L. Rowe, 'The Problem of Evil and Some Varieties of Atheism', in Adams and Adams, eds, *The Problem of Evil*, pp. 126–37. Reprinted from *American Philosophical Quarterly* 16 (1979), pp. 335–41.
10. Rowe, p. 127.
11. Rowe, pp. 129–30.
12. Rowe, p. 131.
13. Wykstra's original response to Rowe is found in 'The Humean Obstacle to Evidential Arguments, from Suffering: On Avoiding the Evils of "Appearance" ', in Adams and Adams, eds, *The Problem of Evil*. Reprinted from *International Journal for Philosophy of Religion* 16 (1984) pp. 73–93.
14. Wykstra, 'The Humean Obstacle to Evidential Arguments from Suffering', pp. 149–50.
15. Wykstra, 'The Humean Obstacle to Evidential Arguments from Suffering', p. 151.
16. Wykstra, 'The Humean Obstacle to Evidential Arguments from Suffering', p. 152.
17. Ibid.
18. Wykstra, 'The Humean Obstacle to Evidential Arguments from Suffering', p. 155.
19. Interestingly, the debate between Rowe and Wykstra has continued. For Rowe's response to Wykstra's initial objection, see 'Evil and the Theistic Hypothesis: A Response to Wykstra', in Adams and Adams, eds, *The Problem of Evil*, pp. 161–7. For Wykstra's response to Rowe's response, see 'Rowe's Noseeum Arguments from Evil', in Daniel Howard-Snyder, ed., *The Evidential Problem of Evil* (Bloomington: Indiana University Press, 1996) pp. 126–50. For yet another round from Rowe, see 'The Evidential Argument from Evil: A Second Look', in the same volume, pp. 262–85.
20. For an example of such speculation about how the world could have been made much better than it is, see David Hume, *Dialogues Concerning Natural Religion* (Indianapolis: Hackett Publishing Co., 1980), particularly the speech of Philo on pp. 67–75. However, Philo (and presumably Hume) does not present these speculations as an argument against belief in God, but only as an argument against natural theology. That is, he does not argue that evil makes belief in God unreasonable, but only that it makes it unreasonable to infer the existence of God from the natural world.
21. *Job* 38:4 (NRSV).
22. *Job* 42:3.
23. For a fine exploration of how particular theistic and even specifically Christian beliefs might bear on the problem of evil in this way, see Marilyn McCord Adams, 'Problems of Evil: More Advice to Christian Philosophers', *Faith and Philosophy* v, 2 (April, 1988) pp. 121–43.

10

Faith and Doctrines Known by Revelation

Much of the philosophy of religion consists of debates about the kinds of issues discussed in Chapters 8 and 9, specifically the existence of God and the problem of evil. However, the great living religions of the world do not merely consist of general beliefs about God. Those religions that do require belief in God embed that belief in a set of concrete, distinctive beliefs about God. For Jews, God is the one who called Abraham and promised to make a great nation of him and who called Moses to deliver God's chosen people from slavery. For Muslims, God is the one who called Mohammed and delivered a final revelation to him. For Christians, God is the one who reveals himself most fully in the life, death and resurrection of Jesus of Nazareth. These kinds of claims therefore raise questions of a different type for the philosophy of religion. How can such specific claims, usually centring around an alleged revelation, be known to be true or justified?

The accounts given of how such particular religious claims can be known will of necessity be as particular as the claims themselves. Muslims may speak of the necessity to have the right attitude of submission to Allah. Buddhists may speak of the necessity to meditate properly and purify oneself of certain kinds of desires so as to see the truths that the Buddha discovered. Some Hindus will speak of the value of mystical experiences that transform the individual and give a whole new perspective on all of life and experience. However, it still may be possible to draw a distinction between different types of approaches to such problems. One distinction that may be helpful is one between rationalist and fideist approaches to the problem.

Rationalist approaches to this second kind of problem try to show that evidence can be given that a particular set of doctrines is true. In the case of a religion that claims its central doctrines are known by a revelation, the evidence often takes the form of evidence that a revelation that contains or implies those doctrines is a genuine revelation from God.

Our discussion of Aquinas in Chapter 4 looked at the type of evidence that might be cited. In that chapter, the focus of the discussion was on what might be called the fideistic dimension of Aquinas' thought, with emphasis on the way that the content of the revelation is above human reason. But there is also a rationalistic dimension in his thought. In particular, Aquinas emphasises the value of miracles as confirming the supernatural origin of a revelation. Miracles, he thought, provide the best evidence that a revelation was genuine.

However, even in Aquinas, this emphasis on what might be called objective, public evidence is not the whole story. In addition to the evidence of miracles, Aquinas mentions that the one who believes in the revelation is moved to believe by 'an inward impulse towards God, who invites him'.[1] Such an 'inner impulse' does not look much like evidence in the normal sense. An account that does not rest belief in particular doctrines on such public evidence might be called fideistic.

Fideistic accounts of this type might be given for a number of different religions. However, each such account will be, as I have said, irreducibly concrete and particular in its details. To illustrate such a fideistic approach, I will once more take Christian beliefs as my example. The purpose of this is not to give an apologetic argument for Christianity but to give a concrete illustration of a fideistic approach to justifying religious beliefs. Someone who knows more about Islam, Hinduism, Buddhism or some other religion might well want to compare my account with the kind of account that could be given for this other faith or faiths. Since Kierkegaard has served as my chief example of fideism, I shall begin with another look at Kierkegaard. I shall also briefly consider some thoughts of the sixteenth-century theologian John Calvin, thoughts that seem consistent with what Kierkegaard says and that suggest a fideistic answer to the question of how particular religious doctrines can be known.

The distinction between general questions about belief in God and more specific questions about the particular beliefs of a religion is paralleled in Kierkegaard by a distinction between two kinds of faith. Kierkegaard distinguishes between faith as a general spiritual capacity to know or be receptive to God and faith as the specific 'passion' that enables a person to recognise Jesus of Nazareth as God incarnate. The generic or 'Socratic' faith, discussed in Chapter 8 in connection with proofs of God's existence and religious experiences, is the outcome of moral and spiritual growth on the part of the individual.[2] However valuable this kind of faith may be as a precursor of faith in the specifically Christian sense, Kierkegaard does not want to confuse the two, or to regard Christian faith as merely a natural development out of the generic kind. It is the specifically Christian kind of faith that allows the believer to come to understand Jesus as Lord and to accept such distinctive Christian doctrines as the Trinity and the Atonement.

KIERKEGAARD'S ACCOUNT OF FAITH IN THE INCARNATION

We saw in Chapters 6 and 7 that on Kierkegaard's interpretation the incarnation of God in Jesus is a paradox to human reason. In what follows, I want to review some of what was said in those chapters, but also to develop the account, by expanding on the positive reasons why a person might come to have faith.

Faith which has a paradox as its object is necessarily above human reason, which does not adequately understand either God or human nature and thus cannot understand how they could be united. However, belief in the incarnation is also against human reason as it concretely, historically exists, since human reasoning is pervaded by a prideful and egoistic character that has trouble accepting its limitations or understanding the character of God's self-giving love. There is therefore a 'natural' negative reaction to the incarnation on the part of human reason, which Kierkegaard expresses in the claim that the possibility of offence is inherent in the encounter of human reason with the paradox.

This negative reaction is not, however, natural in the sense of being inevitable. Rather, Kierkegaard claims that when a person is transformed by the passion of faith, reason and the paradox are on good terms. In this case reason can understand and accept both its limitations and the need to believe what it cannot understand. That rejection of the paradox which he calls 'offence' is not simply a conclusion of cool logic, but the expression of the opposite passion to faith. Reason then is always passionate in one form or another.[3]

What role might evidence play in the formation of faith? From Kierkegaard's perspective, evidence seems to be of small importance. He acknowledges that there must be some 'signs' whereby people would be able to recognise God should God become incarnate, because we can hardly imagine God becoming incarnate to redeem humanity but then making it impossible for anyone to recognise him.[4] Presumably Kierkegaard is here thinking of miracles, fulfilled prophecies, and other things to which traditional evidential apologetic arguments appeal. However, Kierkegaard is not convinced that such signs are an unambiguous plus for faith. The difficulty, he says, is that such things 'may just as well alienate the disciple as draw him closer'.[5]

What exactly is wrong with appeals to miracles and other historical evidence for Kierkegaard? I argued in Chapter 7 that Kierkegaard's depreciation of such evidence is not completely reasonable, even on his own terms.[6] Even if evidence requires faith in order to be recognised and function as evidence, it does not follow that the evidence is not important. However, I think Kierkegaard views evidence as something that is supposed to substitute for faith; evidence for him is something like 'public evidence' that requires no spiritual development or moral virtues to discern.

Kierkegaard has, I think, at least three problems with relying on evidence in this sense. There is first the difficulty that history is the realm of uncertainty; no historical claims can be absolutely certain. The believer, however, is asked to stake his or her life on an historical belief.[7] If such a belief is based on evidence, Kierkegaard thinks that the believer will be 'infinitely anxious', fearful lest some new archaeological dig or literary find may destroy the basis of his or her life. So there is an incommensurability between the significance of the belief in this case and the kind of certainty that historical evidence can provide.

Besides the general uncertainty that attaches to all historical evidence, there is a second problem that is particular to this case. The problem is that it is not clear that any historical evidence could warrant the particular belief in question. One cannot simply reason from the fact that a miracle has occurred to the conclusion that the one who performs the miracle is God incarnate. Perhaps a miracle could support the claim that the miracle-worker is a prophet or has some special authority from God, but there is a large gap between such claims and the Christian belief that Jesus is uniquely divine. It is not clear what particular historical evidence could warrant such a claim.

However, the third problem for Kierkegaard is even greater. This problem is not merely that there is a logical gap between the evidence and the conclusion, such that the evidence is insufficient to warrant the conclusion, but that the conclusion is one that appears to be made improbable by the evidence. This is the heart of Kierkegaard's contention that the incarnation is a paradox. The idea of God becoming a human being is one that human reason cannot understand, and at least for reason that has not been transformed by faith it appears to be absurd. Whatever miracles or evidence someone presented who claimed to be God, Kierkegaard argues that there will always be the counter-evidence that the person claiming to be God appears to be merely an ordinary human being. The fact that the person is in fact a particular human being provides inductive evidence that the person is not divine, since all the other particular humans we have ever met have been non-divine. Suppose my neighbour claims to be God and even does miracles to back up the claim. Apart from suspicions of fraud or other problems the claim might provoke, there would always be the problem of understanding how a particular human being, born at a particular time, could be the divine creator of all things. It is I think for this reason that evidence such as miracles might actually alienate the potential disciple, for if I find it absurd to think that my neighbour might be God incarnate, miracles or other evidence that might be taken as supporting this may be exasperating or irritating to me. I can hardly respond with indifference to someone who makes such a stupendous assertion as a claim to be God. If I do not believe such a person, I will find the claim alienating, and any evidence the person presents may increase the anger or disgust I am likely to feel.

In the final analysis, then, Kierkegaard argues that faith is not the result of evidence. Once more, I think that this claim is not plausible unless we take 'evidence' to mean something like 'public evidence that is indisputable' but that is most probably how Kierkegaard means it. Kierkegaard thinks that some historical testimony is necessary as the *occasion* for faith, but historical evidence is not itself the ground of faith. He defends this claim through a couple of thought experiments. Imagine, he says, an individual who makes it his business to know the historical truth about the one who claims to be God, who is of course Jesus in the case of Christianity.[8] This historical investigator hires hundreds of spies who observe Jesus day and night and make careful and precise records. Would knowing all of this historical information necessarily lead to faith? Not at all, according to Kierkegaard.

The subject of the second thought experiment is a person who has very little historical information about the one who claims to be God. Rather, the second person only comes into contact with the incarnate God when the latter is dying. Would this historical ignorance prevent the second person from becoming a believing disciple? For Kierkegaard, at least, such historical ignorance is not a barrier to faith so long as the moment of encounter with the god is 'the decision of eternity'.[9]

For Kierkegaard faith is 'the condition' that enables the disciple to recognise the God who has become 'incognito' by becoming a particular human being, and this faith is something that is ultimately given to the individual by God. If faith is not present, then evidence is of no value; if faith is present, then even poor historical evidence will be sufficient. '[L]et no innkeeper or philosophy professor fancy that he is such a clever fellow that he can detect something if the God himself does not give the condition'.[10]

This faith is, as we have seen, a transforming passion that amounts to a re-creation of the disciple. How does God give this condition? Kierkegaard does not spell out any mechanism or give any detailed description of the process, but he does emphasise that the gift is one that must be given first-hand. It is the result of some kind of direct encounter with the God who has taken human form. It is through becoming acquainted with the God who has entered human history that people are transformed and acquire the ability to believe.

In Chapter 7 I argued that the characteristics of reason that make faith difficult are the egoism and pride of the reasoner. So it is reasonable to surmise that the transformation of the self that amounts to 'receiving the condition' will be a transformation in which the self humbly recognises its own limits and also begins to care about something other than itself. I think that we can see how an encounter with God in human form could do both of those things. Such an encounter would be humbling because it is by coming to know God's love and compassion that I recognise how selfish and unloving I am. And yet an experience of being loved by God in a deep and profound way might also be the trigger to overcoming that selfishness. Insofar as any purely human analogy can be given, no human experience seems to be more powerful in transforming an individual for good than the experience of being loved deeply.

On Kierkegaard's account faith is a gift; it is something God himself creates in a person. Is there anything a person can do towards acquiring this gift? The only thing that Kierkegaard says the individual can do is to recognise and accept his or her own powerlessness. Here we must recall the discussion in Chapter 7 of the ability of reason to recognise its own limits.[11] Even this ability is dependent on God; it is God's revelation that makes it possible for reason to see its limits. However, this is something that reason confronted with God incarnate can do. But it is not something that reason must do. When reason becomes acquainted with God incarnate, it is given the possibility of recognising its own untruth, but this possibility may be refused. If it is refused, if reason clings to its own autonomy, the resulting attitude is offence.

In any case, for Kierkegaard Christian faith is completely determined by faith in the person of Jesus understood as God. Belief in various Christian doctrines is for him derived from that personal relation of trust. For example, Kierkegaard clearly affirms the Christian view of the Bible as the inspired word of God. However, he gives no evidential arguments for such a view of the Bible. Rather, as he sees it, the Christian perceives the Bible as a personal missive from God – both a love-letter and a revealing critical word – the book that contains the narrative that centres around the story of

Jesus who is my Lord and Saviour, the Pattern for my life and the Redeemer for my life.[12] My attitude towards the Bible is derived from the faith I have in Jesus.

CALVIN AND THE INTERNAL TESTIMONY OF THE HOLY SPIRIT

As noted above, Kierkegaard says very little about how God creates faith in the believer. However, his account has some similarities (as well as some differences) to a view that is prominent among theologians in the Calvinist or Reformed tradition, who do have more to say about this question. Reformed theologians have consistently stressed that knowledge of Christian truth is gained by faith, just as Kierkegaard did, and they would agree with him that faith is not primarily based on rational evidence.

For Reformed theologians, the Bible is a revelation from God (as it is for Kierkegaard) and the question as to how one can know the truths of Christianity rests ultimately on the question as to how one can know the Bible to be true. Here the Reformed theologians and creeds have emphasised the doctrine of the internal testimony of the Holy Spirit. The Belgic Confession, for instance, says that '[w]e receive all these books . . . believing, without any doubt, all things contained in them, not so much because the Church receives and approves them as such, but more especially because the Holy Ghost witnesseth in our heart that they are from God'.[13]

The inspiration for this statement and many others in Reformed creeds is found in John Calvin's *Institutes of the Christian Religion*. In thinking about the truth of the Bible, Calvin has a more positive attitude towards rational evidence than does Kierkegaard. He says that 'so far as human reason goes, sufficiently firm proofs are at hand to establish the credibility of Scripture'.[14] Calvin thinks that one could provide rational arguments for the truth of the Bible *if* one wished to proceed by argument.[15] However, he says that this is the wrong way to proceed; those 'who strive to build up firm faith in Scripture through disputation are doing things backward'.[16] Instead Calvin says that the Christian ought to rely on the internal testimony of the Holy Spirit.[17]

Now what exactly is this internal testimony of the Spirit? One might interpret Calvin to be talking about a kind of inner experience, perhaps one that provides a kind of evidence. However, when looked at in this way, Calvin's account seems fairly weak. It is difficult to know how such an inner experience could be recognised and also difficult to know how it could be authenticated as valid. How can a person know when it is God speaking, and when it is a person's own unconscious or imaginary voices? Since inner experience is quite subjective, the kinds of communal checks that ordinary experiences enjoy would seem to be lacking. I suspect that Calvin is talking not so much about a kind of experience that is to count as evidence, but rather about the same process that Kierkegaard assumes when he claims that faith is something produced in the person by God himself.

Kierkegaard says that faith is something that is given in a first-hand way by God to the disciple.[18] This claim clearly assumes that God is a living reality and that he can be present in some way to the individual. The classical Christian understanding of the continued activity and presence of God in the formation and development of faith is that this is the work of the Spirit of God, who witnesses to the identity of Jesus as the Christ. So I conclude that Calvin, in speaking of the witness of the Spirit, is speaking of the process whereby faith is given to the individual.

In saying that the witness of the Spirit is not to be identified with an experience, I do not mean to deny that it involves experiences, or claim that it is not possible to experience the work of the Spirit. I simply want to maintain that the work of the Spirit in testifying to the truth is not identical with human experience of that work. For Kierkegaard the acquisition of faith is a matter of being transformed, of becoming a different type of person. So also for Calvin, the witness of the Holy Spirit is not merely a matter of providing evidence but of providing what might be called a 'transforming encounter' that thoroughly reshapes the believer.

What is the shape of such a transforming encounter? Of course the process could take various forms. However, one reason for not identifying it with an experience is that the process may well be one that occurs over time. The acquisition of faith does not necessarily occur in a sudden moment, but could be a lengthy affair. The obvious response to this by someone who wishes to consider the experience as evidence is that the evidence could consist of a series of experiences rather than a single one. However, for such a series to constitute powerful evidence, one would think that it ought to be possible to recall all those experiences, and typically this is not possible. It seems more plausible to me to look at the experiences in terms of their effects on the individual. The important thing about such experiences is not whether a person can recall them and see their evidential force, but whether the person who has had such experiences has become spiritually wiser and better able to see the truth as a result.

Typically, an individual encounters the person of Jesus in the words of the Bible or in the sermon of a pastor or the testimony of a friend. The work of the Spirit makes this encounter a living one in which the person is really addressed by God. In the person of Jesus the individual comes to hear God's promises, God's commands, and God's questions. The Spirit helps the individual to reflect on his or her life in the light of that address, and see the richness of those promises, the power of those commands, the appropriateness of those questions. As the individual responds to this address, God speaks in yet more powerful ways. The upshot is that the person comes to see the story of Jesus as the story of God at work in the world. The story takes on the ring of truth because it is seen as the word of God.

Two things have to happen here. First, it must really be God whom I encounter. Secondly, I must recognise that it is God whom I encounter. The claim about the internal witness of the Spirit is a claim that God can realise both conditions. God can speak to me through a hymn, a life, a story. God can create in me an awareness that it is in fact God who is speaking.

EVIDENCE: INTERNALISM AND EXTERNALISM IN EPISTEMOLOGY

Suppose we assume for the sake of discussion that the Reformed theologian is correct in claiming that beliefs are produced in people by the work of the Holy Spirit. Even if we assume this, we may wonder whether believers who have come by faith in this way are justified in their beliefs. To determine whether such beliefs are justified, we must return to some of the basic questions in epistemology or theory of knowledge about the nature of justification and knowledge discussed in Chapter 3.[19]

In the modern period, philosophical accounts of knowledge have typically defined it as justified true belief. If we assume a belief is true, the question as to whether it amounts to knowledge is then essentially the question as to whether the individual is justified in holding the belief. Enlightenment epistemologies for the most part adopted some version of the *classical foundationalist* view of justification discussed in Chapter 3.[20] To review briefly, according to this view some of our beliefs are highly certain – self-evident or at least certain enough to be indubitable. Such certain beliefs are properly basic or foundational. Beliefs that are not properly basic are based on other beliefs which constitute evidence, but those beliefs will in turn require evidence unless they are properly basic.

Most philosophers who have accepted this view of knowledge have held that the evidence should be *internally* accessible to the consciousness of the knower. In order for me to know some proposition, I not only need evidence, but I need to be aware of that evidence, and be aware that it is good evidence for my belief. Such an epistemology is properly termed internalism, since it implies that the individual should be able to tell just by reflection whether or not a belief is justified, since justification depends on facts that are internally accessible to consciousness.

From an internalist perspective, the Reformed account does not look too promising, especially if one adopts the classical foundationalist version of internalism, which stresses that properly basic beliefs must be highly certain. In my version of the story, the Reformed view stresses that what leads to faith is the actual work of the Holy Spirit, and the individual may not be fully aware of this work at all, and certainly not fully certain that experience of this work is indubitable or even highly certain. Of course the individual may have some awareness of the work of the Spirit and those experiences may count as evidence. However, as we have noted, when construed as evidence, this account is not very powerful. What is essential to the Reformed view is not that the individual has experiences that constitute powerful evidence. Rather, the key factor is that the individual becomes transformed in such a way as to make it possible for him or her to grasp the truth.

If epistemological internalism were adequate we would probably find the Reformed account unhelpful. However, twentieth-century philosophers have raised some acute questions about internalism. The major difficulty with internalism is that it assumes that whether a belief is justified is something individuals can determine just by inspecting their consciousness. From an internalist perspective, I see myself as a kind of belief-inspector who has the ability to say whether or not a belief has the proper credentials to count as knowledge. However, it looks as though many of the factors that determine whether a belief amounts to knowledge are not within the control of the individual and not even directly accessible to consciousness.

Of course there is an alternative to internalism, namely the externalism discussed in Chapter 3.[21] The externalist insists that whether a belief amounts to knowledge depends upon many factors that are external to my consciousness and not completely within my control. Suppose I am driving down a highway and see what appears to be a barn. If what I have seen is really a barn, normally one would say I know there is a barn there. What makes this true belief a case of knowledge is described in different ways by different kinds of externalists.

Reliabilists say the belief is justified or warranted because it is produced by a reliable process or faculty.[22] William Alston says it is justified or warranted because the belief is based on what he calls a 'truth-conducive ground',[23] a ground that in most cases actually leads to truth. Alvin Plantinga says that the belief is warranted in case it is the product of a faculty designed to produce true beliefs that is functioning properly in the kind of environment in which it was designed to function.[24] In all of these cases whether the belief has warrant or justification depends on many factors outside my control and that I may not be aware of. What counts is that the process is reliable, or that the ground of the belief is one that in most cases leads to a true belief, or that the belief is the product of a well-designed faculty that is doing its job properly in the right circumstances. I cannot tell that such conditions hold simply by inspecting my consciousness.

In the case where I see the barn, and it is true that the barn is really there, in order for this belief to count as knowledge, lots of other things must be the case. It must, for example, be true that I am not in an abnormal environment. If a Hollywood film company has constructed many barn facades in this area, most of which have deceived me, and I just happen to be looking at the one genuine barn in the area, one might question whether I really have knowledge in this case. To use a yet more exotic example, if my perceptions are all illusory because I am being deceived by a powerful evil demon, or I am really a brain in a vat on another planet being given electrical stimulations that cause me to have certain experiences, then I lack knowledge, even if I accidentally acquire a true belief in a particular case. In general for me to acquire perceptual knowledge, my mental states and eyesight must be relatively normal. But these are things beyond my control, and whether these conditions obtain might not be something I can determine by inspecting my own mind.

For externalism then, knowledge is partly a gift; in theological terms it is not something I can achieve solely by 'works' since my best efforts may be inadequate. Hence the Reformed claim that true religious knowledge might depend on the work of the Holy Spirit, a process that I may not be fully aware of, seems at least possible and consistent with the nature of knowledge in other cases. We are not godlike knowers, but fallible, finite creatures whose knowledge is dependent on many things beyond our control and awareness.

It is helpful here to recall the distinction Alvin Plantinga makes, discussed in Chapter 3, between grounds for a belief and evidence.[25] For Plantinga a true belief that amounts to knowledge must have what he calls 'warrant'. Having evidence for a belief is clearly one type of warrant. However, it does appear that some of our beliefs are not based on evidence in the sense of being based on other beliefs via some process of inference or reasoning. In some circumstances beliefs seem to be formed more or less spontaneously and immediately without being based on any more fundamental beliefs. When I see my wife appear through the door to my home, I form the belief that she has arrived at our home. It is surely the

'new age' thinkers, and perhaps throw in some fundamentalists of various faiths, the likely outcome of such a conclave would be that no agreement on any issue of substance would be possible. In other word, if knowledge requires complete 'objectivity' we will find ourselves becoming sceptics. We cannot achieve such objectivity, and if we could, we could not know anything anyway.

The latter implication is of course a possibility, and plenty of people think that no religious knowledge is possible. However, humans are not generally sceptical about other important areas of human concern. Those who wish to adopt a scepticism about religious matters must show that there is something peculiar about religious matters that entails their scepticism. It is not consistent to urge religious scepticism on the basis of an epistemology that would imply universal scepticism if one is unwilling to follow such a scepticism for other areas of human concern. In any case, scepticism seems a policy of despair; one might see how people might be driven to it if the search for truth is fruitless, but it can hardly be a reason not to seek truth at all.

If the goal of the religious life is truth and not just Meier's interesting game of seeing what people of radically different views can agree upon, then it seems quite possible that some people are simply in a better position than others. Everyone may have 'biases' but some of these may be negative biases that distort and block truth, while others might be 'positive biases' that help people grasp a truth that might otherwise be missed. The Muslim fideist may insist that an attitude of proper submission to Allah's will is a condition for rightly discerning religious truth, including the truth of the *Koran*. The Hindu fideist may want to claim that certain mystical exercises provide the proper precondition for understanding the *Bhagavad Gita*. The Christian fideist may insist that in the case of Christian doctrines that are derived from the Bible, faith constitutes just such a positive bias or enabling condition. Thus the fideist will reject the claim that supposedly neutral historical scholarship provides a necessary foundation for religious beliefs.[28] In any case I am not a 'person in general', but a specific human being. I doubtless have blind spots, but I may also have insights. In any case, it is my life that is at stake, so why should I not follow what seems to me after careful reflection to be truth, even if others do not share my perspective?

I think that it is clear that the Christian fideist may here be joined on a key point by fideists from other religious traditions. Even though the Muslim fideist or the Jewish fideist may disagree with the Christian about the specific nature of the faith or enabling condition that is necessary for gaining the truth, all may agree that detached objectivity is not the way that truth is to be gained. Jon Levenson, a scholar of the Hebrew Bible, for example, argues that members of the guild of critical Biblical scholars should beware of the temptation of seeing themselves as always in a superior position to members of committed religious communities. A claim to cognitive superiority on the part of the critical scholar 'shifts the locus of truth from the practicing community to the nonpracticing and unaffiliated individual'.[29]

With respect to the really crucial religious questions such as the identity and significance of the life of Jesus, the fideist suspects that truly neutral scholarly inquiry is impossible. Even if it were possible, such a stance would not be a help but a hindrance if one's goal is to arrive at truth. Far from it being the case that faith is an evasion of intellectual responsibility, faith may be the indispensable condition for making intellectual progress.

CONCLUSIONS: FAITH BEYOND REASON

We have examined fideism from a number of perspectives. After examining and rejecting the idea of fideism as the rejection of reason, I have examined a number of versions of responsible fideism. I first looked at fideism as the claim that faith without reasons is responsible. Fideism here is the denial of evidentialism. The fideist may deny threshold evidentialism by claiming that faith is not based on evidence at all, or proportionality evidentialism, by denying that the strength of faith must be correlated with evidence. Of course both kinds of evidentialism could be denied as well.

Next, I looked at fideism as the claim that human reason has definite limits and some religious truths are beyond those limits. They are 'above reason' and require faith to be recognised. Finally, I examined fideism in the stronger sense of a claim that reason is not only limited but damaged; hence religious truths are not only *above* but go *against* human reason as it concretely functions, even though such truths may not be against reason as it ideally functions. On this view faith requires the transformation of the person so that the damage done to reason can be repaired or at least alleviated.

Different faiths will of course have different views of just what the damage to reason is and how that damage is to be repaired. Taking Christianity as an example, the damage is due to sin and the faith that has this transforming power is understood by Christians to be a relation of trust in God, a relation that is in turn made possible by a relation to Jesus of Nazareth, understood as the one who makes God known to us. God is both the object of faith on this view and the source of faith. Faith can exist in both general and specific forms, correlating with general trust in God and specific trust in Jesus, but in all cases faith is a transforming passion of trust that enables the individual to grasp truths that would otherwise be opaque or even appear absurd. A reason that is self-critical, open to its own limitations, will be open to the possibility of such a transformation.

Can we have faith without reasons? Is faith above reason? Against reason? We have seen that all may be true, but faith is against reason only in the sense that it runs into conflict with a concrete form of reason that is damaged. Perhaps it is best to describe such a faith as beyond reason rather than against reason, since there is no necessary conflict with reason, but only a conflict with reason that has suffered damage but refuses to recognise this. The metaphor of 'beyond' aptly conveys the thrust of the historic Augustinian view of faith seeking understanding. What is sought is in some sense beyond, or one would not need to seek it.

It might appear that it is reason rather than faith that is 'beyond' in this Augustinian motto, since it is faith seeking *understanding*. However, I do not think 'understanding' in this case is a synonym for reason. Rather, understanding is the goal of human intellectual life. To understand is to know the truth in the way it should be known. From the fideistic perspective, the faith that seeks this understanding is also the faith that heals reason so as to make it possible to move towards understanding. Faith both seeks and enables understanding. Faith enables human beings to move beyond the limitations of finite, fallen human reason.

NOTES

1. Thomas Aquinas, *On Faith: Summa Theologiae*, trans. Mark D. Jordan (Notre Dame, Indiana: University of Notre Dame Press, 1990) 2–2, Q. 2, A. 10, p. 90.
2. See pp. 120–5.
3. See my *Passionate Reason* (Bloomington, Indiana: Indiana University Press, 1992) for a fuller account of what it means to say that reason is passionate.
4. Søren Kierkegaard, *Philosophical Fragments*, trans. Howard V. and Edna H. Hong (Princeton: Princeton University Press, 1985) p. 56.
5. Kierkegaard, *Philosophical Fragments*, p. 56.
6. See pp. 110–12.
7. Søren Kierkegaard, *Concluding Unscientific Postscript*, trans. Howard V. and Edna H. Hong (Princeton: Princeton University Press, 1992) pp. 23–34 and 574–8.
8. Kierkegaard, *Philosophical Fragments*, pp. 59–60.
9. Kierkegaard, *Philosophical Fragments*, p. 60.
10. Kierkegaard, *Philosophical Fragments*, pp. 64–5.
11. See above, pp. 101–6.
12. For Kierkegaard's most powerful account of what it means to read the Bible as God's word, see *For Self-Examination* (published with *Judge for Yourself!*), trans. Howard V. and Edna H. Hong (Princeton: Princeton University Press, 1990), especially the section 'The Mirror of the Word'. For the concept of Christ as 'the Pattern' see *Practice in Christianity*, trans. Howard V. and Edna H. Hong (Princeton: Princeton University Press, 1991).
13. The Belgic Confession, article V, in *The Creeds of Christendom*, iii, ed. Philip Schaff (New York: Harper and Bros, 1877) pp. 386–7.
14. John Calvin, *Institutes of the Christian Religion*, ed. John T. McNeill, trans. Ford Lewis Battles (Philadelphia: Westminster Press, 1960) title of Chp. VIII (p. 81).
15. Calvin, *Institutes*, Chp. VII 4 (p. 78).

16. Calvin, *Institutes*, Chp. VII 4 (p. 79).
17. Calvin, *Institutes*, Chp. VII 4–5 (pp. 78–81).
18. Kierkegaard, *Philosophical Fragments*, p. 101.
19. See pp. 43–7. For a fuller account than that provided in Chapter 3 or in this chapter, see Chp. 9 of my *The Historical Christ and The Jesus of Faith: The Incarnational Narrative As History*, (Oxford: Oxford University Press, 1996).
20. See pp. 41–3.
21. See pp. 43–7.
22. For a clear discussion (and criticism) of various forms of reliabilism, see Alvin Plantinga, *Warrant: The Current Debate* (New York: Oxford University Press, 1993) pp. 182–210.
23. See William Alston, 'An Internalist Externalism', and also other essays in his *Epistemic Justification: Essays in the Theory of Knowledge* (Ithaca, New York: Cornell University Press, 1989).
24. For a full account of Plantinga's position, see his *Warrant and Proper Function* (New York: Oxford University Press, 1993).
25. See Alvin Plantinga, 'Reason and Belief in God', in *Faith and Rationality*, ed. Alvin Plantinga and Nicholas Wolterstorff (Notre Dame, Indiana: University of Notre Dame Press, 1983) for this distinction.
26. See *The Historical Christ and the Jesus of Faith*, Chp. 11, for a fuller account.
27. See John P. Meier, *A Marginal Jew: Rethinking the Historical Jesus*, vol. i (New York: Doubleday, 1991) p. 5. I have slightly modified the terms of the conclave as Meier describes it.
28. For an argument that critical Biblical scholarship does not undermine faith grounded in the witness of the spirit, see my *The Historical Christ and The Jesus of Faith*, Chps. 13 and 14.
29. Jon D. Levenson, 'The Bible: Unexamined Commitments of Criticism', *First Things* 30 (Feb. 1993) 28.

Bibliography

Adams, Marilyn McCord, 'Problems of Evil: More Advice to Christian Philosophers', *Faith and Philosophy* 5/2 (April 1988) pp. 121–43.

Adams, Robert, *The Virtue of Faith and Other Essays* (Oxford: Oxford University Press, 1987).

Alston, William, *Epistemic Justification: Essays in the Theory of Knowledge* (Ithaca, New York: Cornell University Press, 1989).

Alston, William, 'On Knowing That We Know: The Application to Religious Knowledge', in C. Stephen Evans and Merold Westphal (eds), *Christian Perspectives on Religious Knowledge* (Grand Rapids, Michigan: Wm B. Eerdmans, 1993).

Aquinas, Thomas, *Summa Contra Gentiles*, trans. Anton C. Pegis (Garden City, New York: Doubleday and Company, 1955).

Aquinas, Thomas, *Summa Theologiae*, cited from *On Faith: Readings in the Summa Theologiae*, trans. Mark D. Jordan (Notre Dame, Indiana: University of Notre Dame Press, 1990); also cited from *Basic Writings of Thomas Aquinas*, ed. Anton C. Pegis (New York: Random House, 1945); and also cited from Image Books edition (Garden City, New York: Doubleday and Company, 1969).

Banner, Michael, *The Justification of Science and the Rationality of Religious Belief* (Oxford: Oxford University Press, 1990).

Barnes, Barry, and David Bloor, 'Relativism, Rationalism, and the Sociology of Knowledge', in Martin Hollis and Steven Lukes (eds), *Rationality and Relativism* (Cambridge, Massachusetts: MIT Press, 1984).

Barth, Karl, *The Knowledge of God and the Service of God According to the Teaching of the Reformation* (New York: Charles Scribner's Sons, 1939).

Calvin, John, *Institutes of the Christian Religion*, ed. John T. McNeill, trans. Ford Lewis Battles (Philadelphia: Westminster Press, 1960).

Clark, Kelly James, *Return to Reason* (Grand Rapids, Michigan: Wm B. Eerdmans, 1990).

Clifford, W. K., 'The Ethics of Belief', in Gerald D. McCarthy (ed.), *The Ethics of Belief Debate* (Atlanta, Georgia: Scholars Press, 1986).

Coady, C. A. J., *Testimony* (Oxford: Oxford University Press, 1992).

Cupitt, Don, *Taking Leave of God* (New York: Crossroad, 1981).
Davis, Stephen T., *God, Reason and Theistic Proofs* (Edinburgh: Edinburgh University Press, 1997).
Dreyfus, Hubert L., and Paul Rabinow, *Michel Foucault: Beyond Structuralism and Hermeneutics* (Chicago: University of Chicago Press, 1983).
England, F. E., *Kant's Conception of God* (London: George Allen and Unwin, 1929).
Evans, C. Stephen, *Subjectivity and Religious Belief: An Historical, Critical Study* (Grand Rapids, Michigan: Wm B. Eerdmans, 1978).
Evans, C. Stephen, *Kierkegaard's* Fragments *and* Postscript*: The Religious Philosophy of Johannes Climacus* (Atlantic Highlands, New Jersey: Humanities Press, 1983).
Evans, C. Stephen, *Philosophy of Religion: Thinking About Faith* (Downers Grove, Illinois: InterVarsity Press, 1985).
Evans, C. Stephen, 'Kierkegaard and Plantinga on Belief in God: Subjectivity as the Ground of Properly Basic Beliefs', *Faith and Philosophy* 5/1 (1988).
Evans, C. Stephen, *Passionate Reason: Making Sense of Kierkegaard's* Philosophical Fragments (Bloomington, Indiana: Indiana University Press, 1992).
Evans, C. Stephen, *The Historical Christ and the Jesus of Faith: The Incarnational Narrative as History* (Oxford: Oxford University Press, 1996).
Evans, C. Stephen, *Why Believe? Reason and Mystery as Pointers to God* (Grand Rapids, Michigan: Wm B. Eerdmans, 1996).
Foucault, Michel, *Power/Knowledge: Selected Interviews and Other Writings, 1971–77*, ed. Gordon Colin (New York: Pantheon, 1980).
Foucault, Michel, *The Foucault Reader*, ed. Paul Rabinow (New York: Pantheon, 1985).
Green, Ronald M., *Kierkegaard and Kant: The Hidden Debt* (Albany: SUNY Press, 1992).
Hegel, G. W. F., *Philosophy of Nature*, trans. A. V. Miller (Oxford: Clarendon Press, 1979).
Hempel, Carl, 'Problems and Changes in the Empiricist Criterion of Meaning', in *Revue Internationale de Philosophie* 4/11 (January 15, 1950), reprinted in *Classics of Analytic Philosophy*, ed. Robert Ammerman (Indianapolis, Indiana: Hackett Publishing Co., 1990).
Hoitenga, Dewey, *Faith and Reason from Plato to Plantinga: An Introduction to Reformed Epistemology* (Albany, New York: SUNY Press, 1991).
Holmes, Arthur, *Fact, Value, and God* (Grand Rapids, Michigan: Wm B. Eerdmans, 1997).
Hume, David, *Dialogues Concerning Natural Religion* (Indianapolis: Hackett Publishing Co., 1980).
Hume, David, *An Enquiry Concerning Human Understanding*, ed. Eric Steinberg (Indianapolis, Indiana: Hackett Publishing Co., 1993).
James, William, *The Will to Believe and Other Essays in Popular Philosophy* (New York: Longmans, Green and Co., 1897).
Jordan, Jeff (ed.), *Gambling on God: Essays on Pascal's Wager* (Lanham, Maryland: Rowman and Littlefield, 1994).
Kant, Immanuel, *Critique of Judgment*, trans. James Meredith (Oxford: Oxford University Press, 1952).
Kant, Immanuel, *Religion Within the Limits of Reason Alone*, trans. Theodore M. Greene and Hoyt Hudson (New York: Harper and Row, 1960).
Kant, Immanuel, *Critique of Pure Reason*, trans. Norman Kemp Smith (New York: St Martin's Press, 1965).

Kant, Immanuel, *Grounding for the Metaphysics of Morals*, 3rd edn, trans. James W. Ellington (Indianapolis, Indiana: Hackett Publishing Co., 1993).

Kierkegaard, Søren, *On Authority and Revelation*, trans. Walter Lowrie (New York: Harper and Row, 1966).

Kierkegaard, Søren, *Søren Kierkegaard's Journals and Papers*, trans. and ed. Howard V. and Edna H. Hong (Bloomington, Indiana: Indiana University Press, 1967).

Kierkegaard, Søren, *The Sickness Unto Death*, trans. Howard V. and Edna H. Hong (Princeton: Princeton University Press, 1980).

Kierkegaard, Søren, *Fear and Trembling*, trans. Howard V. and Edna H. Hong (Princeton: Princeton University Press, 1983).

Kierkegaard, Søren, *Philosophical Fragments*, trans. Howard V. and Edna H. Hong (Princeton: Princeton University Press, 1985).

Kierkegaard, Søren, *For Self-Examination*, trans. Howard V. and Edna H. Hong (Princeton: Princeton University Press, 1990).

Kierkegaard, Søren, *Practice in Christianity*, trans. Howard V. and Edna H. Hong (Princeton, Princeton University Press, 1991).

Kierkegaard, Søren, *Concluding Unscientific Postscript*, trans. Howard V. and Edna H. Hong (Princeton: Princeton University Press, 1992).

Kuhn, Thomas, *The Structure of Scientific Revolutions*, 2nd edn (Chicago: University of Chicago Press, 1970).

Kuyper, Abraham, *Encyclopedia* Vol. II, cited in Van Til, Cornelius, *The Defense of the Faith*, 3rd ed. (Phillipsburg, New Jersey: Presbyterian and Reformed Publishing Co., 1995).

Levenson, Jon D., 'The Bible: Unexamined Commitments of Criticism', *First Things* 30 (Feb. 1993) 28.

Levinas, Emmanuel, *Totality and Infinity*, trans. Alphonso Lingis (Pittsburgh: Duquesne University Press, 1969).

Locke, John, *An Essay Concerning Human Understanding*, ed. Peter H. Nidditch (Oxford: Oxford University Press, 1975).

Mackie, J. L., 'Evil and Omnipotence', in Marilyn McCord Adams and Robert Merrihew Adams (eds), *The Problem of Evil* (Grand Rapids, Michigan: Wm B. Eerdmans, 1977).

Malcolm, Norman, 'The Groundlessness of Belief', in Louis Pojman, *Philosophy of Religion*, 2nd edn (Belmont, California: Wadsworth, 1994).

Martin, Michael, *Atheism: A Philosophical Justification* (Philadelphia: Temple University Press, 1990).

Martin, Michael, *The Case Against Christianity* (Philadelphia: Temple University Press, 1991).

Mavrodes, George, *Belief in God* (New York: Random House, 1970).

Mavrodes, George, 'Intellectual Morality in Clifford and James', in Gerald D. McCarthy (ed.), *The Ethics of Belief Debate* (Atlanta, Georgia: Scholars Press, 1986).

Meier, John P., *A Marginal Jew: Rethinking the Historical Jesus*, vol. i (New York: Doubleday and Co., 1991).

Myers, David G., *Psychology*, 2nd edn (New York: Worth Publishers, 1988).

Nielson, Kai, *An Introduction to the Philosophy of Religion* (New York: St Martin's Press, 1982).

Pascal, Blaise, *Pascal's Pensées*, trans. W. F. Trotter (New York: E. P. Dutton and Co., 1958).

Penelhum, Terence, *God and Skepticism* (Dordrecht: D. Reidel Publishing Co., 1983).

Phillips, D. Z., *The Concept of Prayer* (London: Routledge and Kegan Paul, 1965).

Phillips, D. Z., *Death and Immortality* (London: MacMillan, 1970).

Plantinga, Alvin, *The Nature of Necessity* (Oxford: Oxford University Press, 1974).

Plantinga, Alvin, *God, Freedom, and Evil* (Grand Rapids, Michigan: Wm B. Eerdmans, 1977).

Plantinga, Alvin, 'Reason and Belief in God', in Alvin Plantinga and Nicholas Wolterstorff (eds), *Faith and Rationality* (Notre Dame, Indiana: University of Notre Dame Press, 1983).

Plantinga, Alvin, *Warrant: The Current Debate* (New York: Oxford University Press, 1993).

Plantinga, Alvin, *Warrant and Proper Function* (New York: Oxford University Press, 1993).

Pojman, Louis, *The Logic of Subjectivity* (University, Alabama: The University of Alabama Press, 1984).

Quine, W. V. O., *Ontological Relativity and Other Essays* (New York: Columbia University Press, 1969).

Ratzsch, Del, *Philosophy of Science: The Natural Sciences in Christian Perspective* (Downers Grove, Illinois: InterVarsity Press, 1986).

Rowe, William L., 'Evil and the Theistic Hypothesis: A Response to Wykstra', in Marilyn McCord Adams and Robert Merrihew Adams (eds), *The Problem of Evil* (Oxford: Oxford University Press, 1990).

Rowe, William L., 'The Problem of Evil and Some Varieties of Atheism', in Marilyn McCord Adams and Robert Merrihew Adams (eds), *The Problem of Evil* (Oxford: Oxford University Press, 1990).

Rowe, William L., 'The Evidential Argument from Evil: A Second Look', in Daniel Howard-Snyder (ed.), *The Evidential Problem of Evil* (Bloomington: Indiana University Press, 1996).

Schaff, Philip (ed.), *The Creeds of Christendom* (New York: Harper and Bros, 1877).

Schleiermacher, Friedrich, *On Religion: Speeches to its Cultured Despisers*, trans. John Oman (New York: Harper, 1958).

Sessions, William Lad, *The Concept of Faith: A Philosophical Investigation* (Ithaca, New York: Cornell University Press, 1994).

Shestov, Lev, *Athens and Jerusalem* (Athens, Ohio: Ohio University Press, 1966).

Swinburne, Richard, *The Existence of God* (Oxford: Oxford University Press, 1979).

Swinburne, Richard, *Faith and Reason* (Oxford: Oxford University Press, 1981).

Swinburne, Richard, *Is There a God?* (Oxford: Oxford University Press, 1996).

Tertullian, *On the Flesh of Christ*, in *The Ante-Nicene Fathers*, ed. Alexander Roberts and James Donaldson, Vol. III (Grand Rapids, Michigan: Wm B. Eerdmans, 1951).

Tertullian, *On Prescription Against Heretics*, in *The Ante-Nicene Fathers*, eds Alexander Roberts and James Donaldson, Vol. III (Grand Rapids, Michigan: Wm B. Eerdmans, 1951).

Torrance, Thomas F., *Theological Science* (London: Oxford University Press, 1969).

Wainwright, William J., *Reason and the Heart: A Prolegomenon to a Critique of Passional Reason* (Ithaca, New York: Cornell University Press, 1995).

Westphal, Merold, 'Christian Philosophers and the Copernican Revolution', in *Christian Perspectives on Religious Knowledge*, ed. C. Stephen Evans and Merold Westphal (Grand Rapids, Michigan: Wm B. Eerdmans Publishing Co., 1993).

Wittgenstein, Ludwig, *Tractatus Logico-Philosophicus* (London: Routledge and Kegan Paul, 1961).

Wood, Allen, *Kant's Moral Religion* (Ithaca, New York: Cornell University Press, 1970).

Wykstra, Stephen, 'The Humean Obstacle to Evidential Arguments from Suffering: On Avoiding the Evils of "Appearance" ', in Marilyn McCord Adams and Robert Merrihew Adams (eds), *The Problem of Evil* (Oxford: Oxford University Press, 1990).

Wykstra, Stephen, 'Rowe's Noseeum Arguments from Evil', in Daniel Howard-Snyder (ed.), *The Evidential Problem of Evil* (Bloomington: Indiana University Press, 1996).

Index